An Absolute Gentleman

An Absolute GENTLEMAN

A NOVEL

R.M. Kinder

COUNTERPOINT

Berkeley

Library of Congress Cataloging-in-Publication Data
Kinder, R.M. (Rose Marie)
    An absolute gentleman : a novel / R.M. Kinder.
        p.   cm.
    ISBN-13: 978-1-58243-388-2
    ISBN-10: 1-58243-388-7
    1. College teachers—Fiction.   2. Serial murderers—Fiction.   3. Psychological
fiction.   I. Title.
PS3561.I429A64 2007
813'.54—dc22
                                                                            2007017932

Cover design by Nicole Caputo
Interior design by Brent Wilcox

Printed in the United States of America

Counterpoint
2117 Fourth Street
Suite D
Berkeley, CA 94710
www.counterpointpress.com

9 8 7 6 5 4 3 2 1

With deepest gratitude to
Kristine Allana Lowe-Martin,
E. J. Ricotta, and Milorad Solujič

CHAPTER 1

Some time ago, two reporters visited me, and I was as open with them as I could humanly be. They came every day for about two weeks and asked maybe a thousand questions. They seemed like nice guys, but just a little edgy. One sloshed coffee around as if I might be somewhere in the dregs. I'm no fool, so I knew they were searching for something no one else had—a slip on my part, an odd phrasing, a gesture, a name. I could have toyed with them, made up corpses buried here and there. But I just answered straight. I try always to tell the truth.

Now, their account of our interviews is in the bookstore, laden with black-and-white photos of me at a typewriter. O-h-h-h, look at the demon creature at work. Don't be misled by the triviality of its habits or the blandness of its gaze. They write that they "occasionally saw glimpses of the monster within." The monster they expected me to be. I remember them pretty well, feature by feature, movement by movement, and they never behaved as if they were dealing with something fearful or distasteful. I liked them overall. They seemed compassionate and kind, and won me over. If they saw something they didn't like, they were looking for it.

The reporters were unfair to me, but I understand that they wanted their book to do well, and I was their material. They shifted me to fit their needs—a kind of early death, dying by hyperbole. They wanted me not to be boring. Be a real monster, they implored silently. Please. Less than a monster will not sell our book.

We may be spectacular in our dreams, but our doings often diminish us.

⟿

They've butchered my mother in their depiction of her. I need to rectify that.

⟿

So, I'm going to tell my own story, my truth. I lived it. I know it best. If anyone's words are going to unravel me, let them be mine. That's justice. Unadorned truth from me to you.

Bluntly—people believe I'm guilty of killing at least eleven women, and perhaps seventeen of them. They think I'm a case of "arrested development," a "child of horrific abuse," a "tortured, twisted psyche."

They're wrong. I am a boring man, an observer. Deviancy in any species fascinates me, particularly if the deviancy is an act of true choice. I would be enthralled with my own nature if it held anything so grounded in will as defiance.

CHAPTER 2

JANUARY 1941

The Georgia farmhouse loomed stark and gray-white in the moonlight. On the second floor, a window opened, and a dark-skinned girl appeared, dressed in a white gown. Mary Blume. She was sixteen, but so slight she might have been only twelve. Now she was agitated, wanting down but afraid to jump, wanting help but knowing better than to call out. She rolled onto her belly, lowered herself as far as she could, and dropped the rest of the way. Then she was up and running. She was quick. Her heavy black hair sliced down her back like silk wings. She thought she was on her way to heaven. On the high wooden bridge two fields beyond, she stopped, confused. The cold air burned her lungs. She gripped her arms beneath her bosom. Her mind was churning. Jesus was now in the water, under the flatsheet ice, and his crown was a partially submerged rock. She knew that wasn't *true*, but she felt like it was. She didn't know what to do. She thought her father might know, but she couldn't remember where he was. She suddenly thought she, too, might be underwater, because the moon was too wavery and everything dark and cold. She stepped nearer the edge of the bridge as if she might jump, then turned and ran. She didn't want to die.

When she reached the black ribbon of highway, the lights of an on-coming car fixed her still, like a wild deer. The car stopped and a voice called out.

"Mary? Mary Blume? What you doing out here like that? You get back to your house."

She knew him and she didn't know him. She darted across the road and into the woods.

"Goddamn crazy loon," the man said. He turned off up the road, speeding to the sleeping Blumes.

Mary ran past the Welker pond, barn, past a scrap heap where discarded box springs glinted moonsilver coils. That frightened her more. She jumped onto the wooden porch, banged her fist against the screen door.

Inside, a young man struggled from sleep and from his strawtick mattress. He opened the front door. There was that she-devil, Mary Blume, in all her psychotic glory. Her black eyes pinned him dead center.

"Tim." She shuddered. "Oh Jesus, Jesus. Dead in the water." She sobbed.

He put his arm around her and pulled her into his disheveled house.

"You shouldn't've come here. What if your dad followed you?"

The dim light glowed over her face and shoulders, the slight swell of her breasts. He curled her to him. He stopped her nonsense-mouth with kisses, warmed her in his bed as he had on other occasions. A little while later he pushed up, lit a cigarette, and said casually, "You should go find Jesus, Mary. He might be dying."

"No."

"It's winter. Cold out there. Poor baby Jesus."

She began to fidget, her fingers picking at the matted blankets and at his hands. He wouldn't hold her now, though. He pulled away from her.

"You better go, Sugarface. The moon's about to fall."

Her eyes startled.

"Yeah honey," he whispered. "You gotta run. Run, Mary. Come on girl. Go. Jesus. Baby, baby Jesus."

She scrambled up.

"That's right, honey. Run."

She did, all alone in her psychotic haze where the figure now behind her was the one she had wanted to reach all along. She ran through the moon-stricken cold fields back to the bridge, was scanning the ice for blood when her father's voice cracked like it fell from the sky.

"Mary! Come here! Now!"

He was at the lower end of the bridge. She backed away.

"Mary!"

Oh, he was terrible and fierce and covered all the mountains and oceans.

She went to him.

OCTOBER 1941

Mary's pains started at two in the afternoon, while she was burning leaves in the barrel at the end of the backyard. She clutched her belly and bent forward, waiting for the bearing-down to subside, then went in the house. She looked immensely healthy, her dark skin flushed over the cheekbones, her eyes clear and lucid. She hadn't had one of her spells in six months, shocked into reality, perhaps, by her parents' death in an automobile accident, by the sudden, utter peace of an empty house. Now, though, she was a little frightened and thought about calling Mr. Sutton to take her to the hospital. He and his wife were members of the church her parents had attended, and they had checked on her since her parents' death.

"Have you seen a doctor?" Mrs. Sutton had asked, but had seemed totally reassured when Mary said, "Yes."

"Well, if you need anything, Mary, you just let me know."

Mr. Sutton had taken her to an attorney. He had showed her how to write checks. There was a lot of money.

"You'll need a car," Mr. Sutton said. But she told him she didn't.

"I'm afraid of cars," she said, bluntly, and he ascribed it to her parents' fatal accident.

"If you want one, I'll help you."

When she needed groceries, she rode into town with the Suttons or she called the store and they delivered. She liked checks. And she liked books.

Now, she removed her clothing and lay on her parents' bed, downstairs. She didn't want to live upstairs anymore. It was like being locked away. Sometimes her father *had* locked her in. Sometimes he was locked in with her, for days.

The pains were far apart. Between them, she thought of things she might need and would rise to get them. A towel, scissors, a pan of water, and a washcloth. A glass of iced tea. Fresh underwear. A robe.

When the pains came close together, she was terribly afraid. What if it ripped her in two? Could that happen? What if it were a monster, all melted into itself? What if it spoke to her?

By the time the baby did come, she was in terror of her own body and lay mesmerized by the moon outside the window, that pendant white flat disc. When the pain crescendoed, she cried out for help, then lay there panting and sobbing, afraid to look. She heard nothing, so she sat up, stared at the writhing slick thing. She grasped its foot, and a cry ensued, a weak, tremble cry. She released it. She remembered she was supposed to cut that cord. She took the scissors, held them firmly and steadily, and lifted the cord to clip it. Then she put them down and tied the cord first. "Almost made a mistake," she said. When she wrapped the baby in the towel, he tried to suck the fabric.

"Oh! Hungry?" She slipped him down, let the tiny mouth clamp on her breast. It hurt and felt good at the same time. "Angel baby," she crooned. "Angel baby, angel love, Momma's little darling." She didn't know where those words came from. Maybe she had heard them sometime in her life and didn't remember. She lay back against the pillow. She felt a tinge of worry over the moon and over even noticing it. "I don't want any trouble," she said pleadingly. "No trouble just for a little while. Okay?"

SUMMER 1942

Mary was calm and dressed well for the hearing. The Suttons testified that she was a good mother. "Oh, she has spells, but she seems to know they're coming on. She takes good care of that baby." They had occasionally taken care of Arthur. Mary would appear at their door, hand them the baby. Later, she would come for him. The social worker had found the home "cluttered with books" but "exceptionally clean." And the baby himself, he reflected good care. The Suttons had taken him to Dr. Phillips in Webster for checkups. There were no marks on the baby. The home had the standard child-rearing paraphernalia and all the necessities—vitamins, cough syrup. The court found that, despite the common rumors that had resulted in the hearing, Mary Blume's personal problems did not stop her from caring for herself or her child. She had been found to have full rights to the estate monies and now she had full rights to Arthur.

NOVEMBER 1942

Mary fed Arthur. He rubbed the green beans on the highchair tray, scooted them onto the floor, and leaned to look at them. She broke a biscuit in two and tore one half into smaller pieces. He squealed for the large half and she gave it to him. He smiled loosely and a piece of wet biscuit fell to the tray.

"You're disgusting," she said. Then, "I'm sorry." She took him from the highchair, mixed bleach water, and wiped down the chair. Now he had smeared green beans over a wider section of linoleum. She picked him up without speaking. She didn't want to say anything ugly, but ugliness was lurking right inside her mouth. She cleaned him with a damp washcloth and carried him into the living room. She set him in the middle of the Persian rug, in the center design. "Stay there," she said, her voice husky and tight. "Stay there, Arthur." He did so. Once he stood up, unsteadily, and seemed ready to try to walk, but he listened instead, his baby face somber, open-mouthed, his eyes on the doorway his mother had gone through. She suddenly appeared there and he sat down. When she came back again, she had with her three filled baby bottles and an open package of crackers. She picked him up with her free arm and carried him upstairs. Though he clasped at her as if he didn't want to be put down, he did want that. She put him in the closet upstairs, turned on the light. "Stay there," she grunted. He shuddered, whimpered. In a moment, he turned and searched for the blanket somewhere behind him. When she came for him again, he had soiled his diapers many times, had cried. The bottles were empty, the crackers gone. She held him on her lap and fed him bananas, peas, mashed potatoes, and bits of chicken. "I do love you, Arthur," she whispered. She kissed his temple, stroked his arms and legs. "That's why I shut you in there, baby. So you won't get hurt."

That's as close as I can get to my beginnings without conjecturing too far. My mother left only scraps of information. Her history was in her mind.

I suspect all three of the men mentioned in the foregoing were bastards, not counting myself. At least one of them was.

CHAPTER 3

When I moved to Mason, Missouri, in the late summer of my fiftieth year, I intended no one any harm. I like people. We're all caught in the same maelstrom of patterns and it's better to sympathize with one another than to compete. So, no, I wasn't looking for new territory. I've never *had* a territory. I was looking for a new start, a place where I could stay. I wanted a job with some permanence, a little prestige, and maybe some winning students. I didn't expect friends. They had never been a part of my life.

Mason had advertised that rarity of rarities—a creative-writing position, possibly tenure-track. My current contract was ending, I wasn't happy, and the paper was lying open to the Mason advertisement when I picked it up. On such signs do lives turn. I sent the best vita I could compose and even sent copies of the reviews of my first book. I guess I impressed them; but then, perhaps I'm the only one who applied. The chair of the department called and set up two telephone interviews. Two weeks later, they told me I had the job. They asked for me. They got me. Simple as that.

I was determined to give myself the best chance at Mason. I read up on the area. The "Heartland of America," their literature boasted, as if calling it so made it so, as if in the center of America the earth pulsed. Sickening idea, really, if one dwells on it. Pictures of the region were enticing, though—woodlands, lakes, rolling hills, highways dappled with leaves and sunlight, sweeping blue skies, fair-skinned girls, all too plump and too pretty. I wanted to go, to settle into a pleasant community and be accepted.

If I could read natural signs as accurately as I wish, as some baser animals are able to do, I'd have known that Mason was probably going to be a world of hurt and sorrow. Rain pelted down when I crossed the line into Missouri. The sky flared warning in booming yellow streaks. Go back, Arthur Blume. I wouldn't pull over and wait it out, because I know you can't conquer fear by running. You have to learn that you'll survive. I stopped when, according to my watch, it was time to stop, no earlier than 8:00 p.m.

Schedules are the most comforting habit humans have formed.

The weather eventually cleared, and I took my time driving northeast to Mason. I wanted to know the area, to absorb the community. You can tell a lot about people by the country around them. It seemed a soft landscape in many ways. Big Apple Creek. Little Apple Creek. Deer Crossing. Goddard's Ridge. The Missouri River—dark, roiling, full to the height of the banks. Some young saplings had been swallowed up by the recent rains.

I recall seeing a young woman standing near the bank, eating an apple. She had a paper sack in her left hand and I assumed she had stopped for lunch. It was a lazy day for her, too. Maybe promising. The trees behind her were so dense they made the air seem green. It was a lovely scene. I pulled off at the next exit and drove back. There she was, still staring at the dark water, then turning as she heard my car approaching. So, her little mind probably considered, should she leave now, immediately, because a strange man had driven in?

The next day, I reached Mason itself. I had hopes. The town was about three miles square, with a cemetery near the highway, a small rose garden maintained by the proverbial and pervasive Optimist's Club, and five plastic parks—swings, monkey bars, merry-go-rounds. All empty. The downtown district was one street, long and narrow, dipping down to railroad tracks and up to the one decent structure in town. It looked like a stone cathedral, something out of a medieval past. The dome, some kind of highly polished stone, reflected the sky, and because of that seemed in motion—a gentle swirling blue and white, a world within a world. That did intrigue me, and I drove by all the other businesses, with their flat, dark facades, to park near the structure and to read the legend. It was the courthouse. Of course. It had been built by community volunteers over a period of five years. I studied it, enjoyed it, and was trying to discern the features of two statues on either side of the dome when I felt and heard someone behind me.

"Best thing we got."

I turned around. A sheriff's deputy stood there, lighting a cigarette. He was a friendly-looking soul, tall and sloppy-fat, with thick, loose lips, blue eyes, and hands that could break bricks. "I was wondering about the statues," I said. "Those rods in particular."

He squinted up. "Used to hold bells. Been about, oh, six years, I guess. They took the bells off." He rambled on about the bells being noisy on windy days, and people complaining about the sound and the cost of upkeep. "They cracked about once every other year," he said.

A breeze swept over us, blew a scrap of paper against the legend's metal frame. He picked it up. He was an orderly man, who obviously didn't like things out of place. It was pleasant talking to him, scanning his name tag, his features, meeting his direct gaze. I usually prefer not to meet looks head-on. His name was S. Dyer. "Shirley Dyer," he said, and smiled.

"You get teased about that?" I asked.

"Not much." He laughed and I understood. Size matters.

I checked into a motel overlooking a pond. Just at sunset I walked around the upper rim. No geese or ducks swam on the calm surface. It held only a passive, inverted sky, undisturbed by ripple or movement. The stars and moon were wavery. I like small universes where we don't expect them, parallel structures. I returned to my room. I listened to the news. A woman's torso had just been found in the Missouri River, the sixth such mutilated body in three years.

"Poor devil," I said to the empty room. So much for the conservative heartland of America. But I didn't despair. A place, like a creature, can have dual natures.

I lay reading my latest manuscript, *Ghosts*, until it was time for me to sleep. I loved that book. I wanted it published so desperately that I didn't dare *think* about it. It would stir me up like a fire and I'd be miserable for days. I had to teach myself patience, patience. I turned out the light and put my hand on the typed pages as other people do a pillow or a person. I woke once and had to turn on the bedside lamp. The newscast had apparently entered my subconscious and I was tense anyhow, from the move itself. I often sleep with a light on. I used to suffer from night terrors.

Overall, my arrival fit the pattern. I didn't *set* it. I can't cause storms, or put statues on buildings, or decide the movements of law officers, or arrange telecasts. I just breathe, think, work, move. Hope.

CHAPTER 4

Parents often confine their children when necessary, so I don't think my mother was unusual in that way. I imagine she didn't have much choice or didn't know about any choices. We act according to the resources we have. When she felt her world changing, she protected me as best she could. By at least age two or three, I knew not to call for her. She would come eventually. The closet was my caretaker and my babysitter. I didn't become *fond* of it, just comfortable. I've read that even pain becomes familiar and bearable, sometimes even welcome. It's an odd assurance of one's place. The closet was deep and wide, storing only old coats, and their pungent smell became pleasant. In the corner, three folded blankets awaited my arrival. I guess she washed them from time to time, during her good periods. And I had a small wooden chair. I remember that it had no paint. The arms were spindled, and I often traced the grooves while I waited for her to appear. After I learned to count, I discovered there were thirteen grooves on each arm and on each leg; the back carving had twenty-four semicircles in all and resembled a face, fat and smiling, if I closed my eyes. The disparity in odd and even numbers later troubled me. It was a deliberate imbalance in the very making of the chair.

Sometimes I heard her return from a walk, or visit, or trip to town (or wherever she went or thought she went), and I would listen intensely for her movements toward the stairway. Sounds, you see, become directions when they're all you have. If she would move at all, I knew exactly where she was. If she stayed in the kitchen, I knew she was eating and reading, and might be a long time in coming for me. She held the book with her left hand, turning the pages with a thumb, while she ate with her right. I can read like that, too, but I've made a point of not consuming words with food. Appetites should be kept separate so you know what they are. Many times she would come upstairs and sit outside the closet door. I worried then. I couldn't get the clues.

"Are you in there, Arthur? Do you want to come out? Will you be good? Shall I read you a story?"

Once, perhaps to punish her in my weak, childish way, I said, "No," that I didn't want to come out. She was silent. Then I heard her weeping. That's a wrenching sound, from any human being, or should be. "Yes, I do," I said. "I do want out." She opened the door and I saw my mother's other face, that stranger, gaunt, with eyes shadowed like bruises and yet burning, the mouth a thin red slit. "Then come out," she said, and I scooted back under the coats to the far corner. She left me alone. She forgot to lock the door, but I didn't leave the closet.

True tales: I knew a woman once who took her son for a stroll. They lived on land that was planted only when neighboring farmers leased land from the mother. It was an attractive farm, cut through with a creek and spotted with walnut, oak, hickory, and other huge trees. A narrow wooden bridge spanned the creek. There were no side railings. Sometimes, when the mother paused at the highest end, the little boy held his breath.

This particular day, she didn't stride onto the bridge at all, but walked under the trees shading the creek. The boy was careful to stay a little behind her. When she moved into a clearing, he followed.

"Look there," she said, and pointed at vines growing up the base of a trunk. He saw the leaves trembling in the breeze. He didn't know what he was to respond, so he said nothing.

"You see how that vine grows around the tree? It's choking the tree, that's what it's doing." She stared at him as if to verify that he understood. She shook her head. "Just choking the tree."

He nodded.

"Someone should pull it off, shouldn't they?"

He nodded again.

"You think you could do that?" She sat down, leaned back on her arms. Her black hair hung straight and heavy almost to the ground. She smiled at him. "You want to do that for me? Pull off those vines?"

He got up immediately and walked to the tree. He tried to grip the vine, but it had rooted in the bark. Still, he managed to break the vine in places and to strip it of leaves. He moved on to other trees as she directed him to do.

Later, in the kitchen, when eruptions burned on his entire body and swelled shut his eyes, she said, "Guess that was poison ivy you got into."

She made a paste of baking soda and water and dotted it all over his naked body. "You're a sight," she said. "A real mess."

On another summer day, she pointed at a brown ribbon emerging from beneath a creek rock. "Water moccasin," she said. "Poisonous snake. Really likes little kids." The boy went rigid in her arms. The ribbon undulated in the water, finally disappeared from his sight.

The boy was uncomfortable with her gripping him so tightly, but he didn't move at all. He hoped she would turn back home, but she didn't. She slipped her shoes off and stepped into the water. She waded to the flat rock where the snake had emerged, and set him down feet first. He kept his hands locked behind her neck, but she unfolded his fingers. Then she waded back to the bank and squatted, resting her elbows on her knees. She wore a light yellow sundress, and the cut of the dress's front revealed her shoulder bones.

He stood there a long time, maybe hours. He could see rocks on the bottom, some dark green as if a miniature world were under there, with soft grasses and waving trees. He waited for ribbons to curl up over the edge of the rock and hurt him. He knew then she'd take him home. When she tossed a pebble near the rock, he wet his pants.

"We can go home when you're ready," she finally said.

A few moments later he stepped into the water and walked out. That, too, was my mother. I amused her. And she loved me.

⟵

Sometime during those years, Mr. Sutton died. My mother said he died of a heart attack, but she later remarked he had fallen into the pond and struck his head on a stone. She reported this as if she had read it somewhere. She was eating a slice of bread at the time, pinching off small pieces from the center out. My mother was a slight woman, almost nothing. Mr. Sutton was such a large man, but he had been displaced and she hadn't. I didn't understand how these facts were related, but knew they were.

Mrs. Sutton continued to help my mother. Mrs. Sutton, horse-faced, stupid woman. She was by common standards a good woman, soft-voiced and charitable. She had a dog, a herder of some kind, black and white, with two-colored eyes. I never had a dog, though I wanted one.

—

Storms were frequent in our Georgia countryside, and they were fierce from my upstairs room. Lightning crackled and flared all the windows at once, as if it surrounded the house. I wasn't supposed to go downstairs after bedtime, but I couldn't help it. One night I spent in the living room, in the center of the rug. Another just outside her bedroom door. Another time, when the house shuddered from the wind, when windows rattled and glared like sudden daytime, I flew down the stairs, across the rug, and into her room. I threw myself into the deep chair opposite her bed and sat panting, knees drawn up and shielding me from whatever beset the house. My skin was electric, humming from terror. I thought she hadn't wakened. But then she sat up, very slowly, too slowly.

"Momma?" I whispered.

She pulled the sheet of her hair forward and held a fan of it over her mouth. Her voice came broken and hoarse. "What do you want, little boy?"

I was out of the chair and running for the door before she finished.

She caught me. "Oh, Arthur. It's just me." She laughed and pulled me back to bed with her. "You're so easy to scare. You've got to get over that, honey." She stroked my chest with just the tips of her fingers. She called it "tickling." When I was tired and not wary of her, it could ease me into sleep, as if her fingers wove me into safety. She said even when I was a baby I would lie still to that stroking. "You can't be afraid of the weather, Arthur. There're too many other things to watch out for. You got to get brave." She leaned over and kissed me on the lips. I couldn't see her eyes at all. Then she scooted away, so we weren't even touching. Lightning snapped and I saw her watching me. I wasn't sure what to do. In a little while she took my hand and I fell asleep. I woke once because she was touching me again.

━

I once saw a special on a crazed chimpanzee, female, a new mother. She couldn't care for her offspring. She would carry the baby around in her left arm, just under the teat, and occasionally shake the baby, urging it to nurse. But she didn't hold the baby quite close enough, and didn't urge it *right*. The researchers interfered with the third offspring. They took it away to feed it and that inept mother grieved. You could see it in her expression, her posture, the curving of her empty arms. She *longed* to feed that baby. She just couldn't get her desire and her nature to blend.

Another chimpanzee female was a marauder in a natural setting. Worse, actually—a cannibal. She ripped away the newborns of other chimps *and ate them*. She taught her own offspring to do the same. That mother chimp had flat brown eyes. No expression at all. It was a terrifying film.

These creatures weren't alike. They were both aberrants, but one was more horrendous. Both had no choice, but one seemed to *want* choice.

CHAPTER 5

I've always believed there's an order beyond any system that science can uncover, one similar to the structure of atoms and galaxies, but invisible, like an infinite web stretching over the universe. We see bits of it every now and then and we try to intuit the whole. But we're so damned *tiny*. What do we think we can see? An insect sees the spider's web, feels it entangling him tighter, tighter, cloying, immobilizing. Beyond it? The spider, the tree, webs of birds, mammals—prey and predator. The insect doesn't *know* this, that web leads to web, leads to web. One of them is going to get you. In fact, you're *in* one of them already.

And maybe the structure is inverse, too. I recently read about a scientist who has captured antimatter. It's all around us, he says, but difficult to capture. Maybe we've seen it. Maybe we've seen black holes, had one sweep through us. Maybe galaxies die behind our eyes and cause our moments of abysmal, complete despair. Then, though still ignorant, we would at least be grand.

⟵

I looked at Mason apartments for three days, and they were all structured by the same architects, convenience and money. Then, not too far from the campus, I found this four-storied brick beauty—stained-glass windows, arched panes, double oak doors. The manager let me roam the building and I was delighted at every turn. It was like walking into a rich past. At each upstairs landing a window cast multicolored light. I walked down halls lined with dark wainscoting and rose wallpaper. The carpet still held a faint pattern of rose flowers and winding green vines. I felt at home, though I'd never lived in such a place. My right hand itched for a cane. I needed to be wearing a suit, a top hat, have a cloak sweeping behind me. It was a winning atmosphere.

I stopped before an open door. Inside, a young man, seated cross-legged on the floor across from a proper mirror, sketched himself with charcoal. I could see his features in the mirror and in the sketch. It was good work. The whole paper was shades of gray, like wind-driven rain, but with the darker lines gradually coalescing into a brooding face—strong jaw, high cheekbones, slightly sunken cheeks, round, wide-spaced eye sockets, black pupils with a spark of light.

"It's an unkind likeness of yourself," I said. "You've coarsened your features."

His mirror reflection glanced at mine. "I know." Above his face, mine was sallow and sagging, my heavy brows making my eyes just shadows. He returned to his work, as if I weren't still standing in his doorway.

I had liked his response, the way he owned his craft, both the intent and the result.

His name was Jack Goff. I saw the name firmly written under the apartment number. It suited him.

I rented a room on the third floor, a corner unit that allowed me to see the front and side lawns and the globe lights marking the entrance. The next day I drove to used furniture and antique stores. I bought deep, soft chairs with wide side-wings, dark, rich fabric, burnished wood, Persian rugs. Even the finishing touches I chose carefully to blend with the place: tapestry wall-hangings; a miniature three-legged clock with inlaid blue enamel; mother-of-pearl catch-all dishes; a rack of old pipes with humidor, though I don't smoke.

I encountered young Jack again when the furniture was being delivered. He helped, and I paid him against his generous protests. We talked for a few minutes and that was enjoyable. Afternoon sun through the room, dust-haze. He was an art major, he said, and would be taking writing courses.

"Then you'll be my student."

That rattled him. Gone was the equality he had felt, but not for long. He reemerged. He was a beautiful young man, a head taller than I, lean, with that Russian wild black hair that won't lie down, with fair skin flushed from energy or expectation.

I told him about my first book, *Fathers*, and showed him a copy.

He turned it over, scanned the photograph on the back, then opened it to read the date of publication.

"I was about your age," I said. "Maybe a year or two older."

"I write poetry myself."

"I'll be teaching that, too."

"But this is fiction, right?"

"My strength is fiction. But I write and teach both fiction and poetry. Don't worry. I'm a good teacher."

Already I was defending myself. I loaned him the book and he left. I almost regretted having invited him in. He had come, judged, found me tolerable, and left superior. And I had orchestrated the whole affair. It happens. We invite challenges to our right to be alive. That's why I prefer not to take action on my desires, but only to act spontaneously, from outside stimuli. If I don't cause, but only react, then I'm not guilty of anything, especially my own pain.

⟵

My first day at the office I met those persons, other than students, who would be most important to me in Mason. I now find that odd but reassuring, as if they were all lying in wait for me to appear so they could slip into action. All these inverse possibilities circling around Arthur Blume. Oh, where do I belong? And me? And me?

Imagine this: a round dumpling woman, between sixty and eighty, with thin brown hair curled into loose ringlets and tied with a pink bow at the very top, like a doll; a pink print dress with a white cummerbund; white stockings, black slippers.

I had the feeling that someone was watching me, and I turned just at the entrance to the English Department. There she was, hands clasped at her waist. Demure and intense. She peered at me steadily for perhaps half a minute. Then she *curtsied* and disappeared through a doorway to her right. I had never seen an actual curtsy. I had never seen a woman like her in a university setting. In books, yes. Old paintings. Christmas scenes. But in the English Department of a university? No.

She seemed a good omen, bringing a little magic into a difficult day. It isn't easy, you know, being the "new man" in a temporary position, particularly when one is fifty and his last major publication occurred when he was in his twenties. You can't be "up and coming." You're the bottom man, everyone knows it, but no one says it.

In a backwater university, though, a person with decent behavior and one solid publication has a chance.

I went on about my business, but in a lighter mood. The department secretary was Margaret Felling. I'd known her kind at other campuses—out of the way, everyone, no nonsense here, I will barrel through this piece of turf, knock every dissenter out of the way with my voluminous bosom, scowl them into compliance, stamp them down and dirty. *Follow all the fine print, Mr. Blume, and we will be okay.* She plied me with regulations, forms, and brochures.

A few feet to my right a man watched us, and I found my eyes drawn to him as well. He was no taller than I, 5'8" at most, but bony, with disproportionately wide shoulders and a skull-like head. He was ruddy, that rough redness of a fair-skinned man too much in the sun, and his eyes seemed mismatched with that fairness. They were a flat black, dull, as though we didn't register with him even though he was fixed on us. I nodded toward him and he didn't return the gesture. So much for him. When the secretary requested that I move my pre-shipped books to my office as soon as possible, he spoke. He had been attending us all along.

"Best do everything she says, or your syllabi won't get copied in time. Margaret rules the roost."

Then he closed his eyes, tilted his head back, and held two fingers of his right hand against his left wrist. He was taking his pulse. The secretary ignored him, so I assumed this was common behavior. I also assumed he wanted attention.

"Are you all right?" I said.

He maintained his pose. I could have been offended, but I wasn't. I waited. His breathing was very slow. When he lowered his head and opened his eyes, he was visibly very relaxed. He took a second more to focus on me.

"You said something?" he asked.

"If you were all right."

"I was meditating. It's a handy tool, at the least, and especially helpful around here." A sideways glance indicated the "here" referred to Margaret. "You must be the new creative writing fellow."

"Yes."

"I'm Paul Harper. Welcome to the zoo."

He walked past me, down a short hall and into an office, and closed the door.

"Is he a professor?"

"Oh yes," Margaret said, nodding. "He's the brain of the department."

Harper's door had opened a little. He stood far enough back to see a sliver of us, then came forward as if for my benefit, and eased the door shut again. Apparently he liked closing things.

I retrieved my books, unpacked Faulkner's works and placed my own slender volume next to his many—an urge toward greatness by proximity. I heard a shuffle and swish and knew immediately who it was. The flounce of her filled the doorway. She held her hands at her waist, one cupping the other.

"I hope I'm not interrupting," she said.

"No. Not at all."

"I wouldn't want to interrupt you. You being a doctor and all. I've been told not to bother the professors."

"No. I'm not a doctor."

She took one step forward. "But you *are* the new professor."

"Assistant professor, yes. Arthur Blume. Mr. Blume."

With another quick bob, she was fully in the office, extending one white, dimpled, but firm hand, and leaving the impression of fluttering, though she actually stood before me and simply twisted herself a bit, like a kid who isn't shy but wants to appear so.

"Nada Petrovich. I'm a student. Well, I do research sometimes, and other work, but I'm not anybody grand, no professor or anything. Have you met anyone? Someone should be here to meet you."

"I've met the secretary, and Dr. Harper."

"What did you think of him?" A brief, sharper look from her, like a flash of assessment.

It was a clue I missed.

I shrugged. "Pleasant enough."

"He burns incense, so if you smell something, the office isn't on fire."

Up close, she was obviously old, but somehow still lovely. Her skin had the fragile, pale transparency of fine rice paper. Tiny veins spidered her cheeks. They weren't ugly veins, just noticeable, as if she were ripe, near bursting. She had a cupid-bow mouth, tinted pink. Her eyes were dark blue—plum-colored—and quick. Even as she spoke, they darted around the office as if she were looking for something specific. There was something merry about her, soft and lighthearted, but also something disconcerting—perhaps the very activeness of those eyes in a fat and aging body.

I liked her.

"They should have been here to meet you," she stated emphatically. "No excuses."

I explained that no one knew I'd be at the office today and that I didn't like fanfare or formality. "No one owes me anything," I said. She seemed satisfied with that, though I could tell she held a grievance against "them," who had been so derelict in their duty. She proceeded to urge comforts on me, a cup of coffee, a sandwich, a sweet roll. She even offered me an extra bookcase.

"I could find you one," she said, "only you mustn't tell Margaret."

I turned down that favor. But I let her do the rest. She flurried in and out for the next hour. Bookends. A feather duster. She wiped my desk down with wet paper towels, then dried it. She didn't talk *to* me, just that murmuring chatter women do as they clean, sing-songy, lulling. Deceptive.

Before she left, she dropped the blinds and adjusted them so the light sliced across the room. "It will get hot in here later," she said. "If you need anything, put a note on my door. I don't have a mailbox. I'm the only one who doesn't. Of course, I'm not complaining."

"And why don't you have one?"

"Margaret says I work for the department and she's the main secretary, so she gives me my work. Don't tell Margaret if you want me to do something, okay?"

"Okay."

"Because she won't tell me. She wants to make me look bad."

She patted me on the shoulder. Three light little taps. Then she was out the door, turning girlishly in the hall to smile at me and bustle on.

Three light little taps. Tap. Tap. Tap. I liked being patted like that. Such a simple, human touch.

⟵

Carl Loeffle sought me out next. He was lank and loose like a folding wooden doll, kind-voiced and ugly, a boyish, intellectual

Ichabod Crane. He seemed to feel slightly guilty that Nada had had to tell him I was on campus. "What'd you think of our old girl?" he said.

"Charming. A real intrigue."

"Oh, Nada keeps us going, that's for sure. She likes to chide. At least me. Of course, I probably ask for it."

He gave me a brief tour of the English Department, stopping finally at his own office. He had pictures of Emily Dickinson on the wall (she was an exceedingly homely woman, and actually *stank*, or so historians say, from some disease). Carl had books open everywhere, even on the floor. I recognized his type. He was the kind of man who was totally attentive in your presence and then forgot you the moment you were out of sight. But genuinely, wholeheartedly, automatically, and immediately fond of people. It shone from him like a beacon. I've known two or three people like him. They wished me well or perhaps just wished me no harm, but they had other lives and forgot mine. Encapsulated, ineffectual good.

⟶

Then came Grace Burch. I should have recognized her nature. But she was skilled in artifice, as women are. They have centuries of pretense behind them, and perhaps that has been necessary to their survival.

I saw her at the end of the hallway, handing Nada a cumbersome armload of books.

"Please wait," she called. Her little heels clicked against the tile. "I won't keep you but a minute."

She was diminutive, the same height as Nada but delicately thin, with black hair cut blunt short—only a springy natural wave saved it from the bowl-cut look of another era. She was childlike and animated, like a windup toy that's going to run down fast. She was lovely. Absolutely. A tiny, chiseled face, red lipstick, little mascara, if any. Black, intelligent eyes. She made those little gestures of a woman who has been rushed—adjusting her purse on her arm, brushing back her hair. "Thought I'd introduce myself before you left," she said. "Or maybe you'd like to have dinner? Has anyone shown you around Mason? Poor man—new in town and no one's here."

"I've been here a few days. There's not much to see."

"Oh, a keen-eyed, honest man. Let me take your arm."

She actually took it and leaned into me as she led us down the empty hallway toward the elevator. "I dislike stairs," she said, "although descending them on some occasions can be fun." I thought she alluded to a world of ballrooms and great decorum. I also took the statement as an invitation of sorts, though I didn't understand it.

She lamented, brightly, Mason's meager offerings in the area of entertainment. She drove us to the Crossing, Mason's "best dining establishment," a bar-restaurant lined with photographs of historic buildings, movie stars, and horses. From two corners of the ceiling hung large television screens. She chattered, ordered coffee, opened the menu at least three times. "Are we very hungry or not?" she said. "Shall we do this little business a favor and order their best? Or punish them and have an appetizer? Arthur?"

She ordered halibut. She chain-smoked. She left dark red rings on the tips of each cigarette. She took out a pill holder and sorted among the pastels, then popped a pale yellow one in her mouth.

"Are you ill?"

"That was a vitamin. I forgot it earlier."

I didn't ask about the other pills, since, in spite of what she said, the yellow one had not been a vitamin. She may have needed to slow herself down at times.

On the television screens above us both, a series of women's faces flashed, followed by pictures of a river, then white-draped bodies, then a dismembered leg.

"You've a serial killer here," I said. "I'm surprised, in this part of the country."

I recall that she wasn't concerned in the least. She glanced at the screen. "Oh, that crazy guy. Whoever he is, I hope he stays out of Mason. What, though," she sipped her drink, "could bring him here? Even murderers probably have taste."

She was a judgmental woman.

She had symmetrical circles around her throat, two of them. They come from a particular exercise women do, a stretching of the neck while they grin widely. It tautens the muscles. A knife could be inserted on one side and split that seam wide open. Just there. From there to there. Iva Sutton had grinned in that fashion, a memory that made me feel more comfortable with this new colleague, willing to listen, like reading a book around someone else's words, adding your own ending.

At one point in my evening with Grace, I said, "You have lovely skin." It was certainly true, and it pleased her.

"Thank you," she said.

When she drove me back to my car, she was calmer, having, I supposed, assured herself of my availability. Before I shut the car door, she leaned across the seat.

"Would you like to drive into Kansas City Friday evening?" she asked. "My treat."

"You don't need to do that."

"My pleasure."

"Then mine as well." I bent toward the window again. "What were those books you gave Nada?"

"They're overdue at the library."

"She returns them for you?"

"She likes to do things like that. She used to work over there. She erases all my little margin scribblings, too. Then she tells me I shouldn't mark up things that aren't mine. She enjoys correcting people."

I didn't believe that anyone enjoyed doing others' drudge work. I still don't believe it. It's something else they enjoy, the power of the underling, knowing about dirty linen and secret scribblings.

"Be careful driving home," I said.

I acquiesced to Grace, which is always my way. I had no designs on her. Every place I've gone there's been one waiting to reel me in. It's America's favorite pastime. I didn't really mind. There's something terribly sad about an aging woman, especially Grace's kind. A fraying butterfly. Flapping ragged wings. Come love me. Come love me.

It was Nada I thought about most at the end of the day. What a delightful old gal. Curtsying. Bustle whoop-de-doo—this place will get clean, let me help you, have a cookie. I had never known anyone like her. She was comforting.

No one had mentioned my first book, but that wasn't unusual. Probably no one had read it or would read it. I understood their reasoning. They just needed a teacher, someone not too threatening.

They had hired me like a shot in the dark. Fish and catch what you can. Was he any good, this Arthur Blume? What did it matter? The fellow might be temporary. They could live with the devil himself for a short time.

The next morning I woke in that most miserable of conditions, still paralyzed by dream and conscious enough to know it. I can't cry out, open my eyes, move one hand, one finger. I struggle against myself and I can't win. It's like being caught in a dead body, unable to set the spirit free. I know this is a normal state, but it doesn't feel normal. A current researcher says it's just that we wake up before we're supposed to. It's a universal experience with a long history. He thinks it gave rise to beliefs in visits from demons and witches. "The hag came last night," people reported, "sapped my strength" or "sucked my breath." The experience caused charges against innocents, caused burnings, stonings, deaths. All from a natural reaction of the human body—the spirit waking while the body lies sleeping.

I emerged drenched, with ragged breath, to the sounds of rain and light thunder. But it was a slow rain, with sparse, fat droplets. It wasn't frightening. I wasn't happy, though. I was slow and heavy. Happiness is such an elusive thing.

I spent the day preparing *Ghosts* for resubmission. It had already been rejected by eighteen publishers, but I knew it was a good book. I simply had to keep trying. One reader had written, "Need more about the ghosts." Another had written "nice" beside some passages and I reread each of those sections. They *were* good.

You see, I have no illusions about my capabilities as a writer. I'm talented, yes, but not deeply so. I'm also erratic. Every now and then I'll stumble into a scene so vivid I forget I wrote it, or a voice so engaging I find myself listening more than writing. But I can't count on that talent or draw on it. I have to wait and wait for whatever's in me to dart out for a while.

I sent out the cleanest sixteen copies. I wanted some good possibility hanging in the wings before the semester started. We have to create little rewards for ourselves.

CHAPTER 6

My third year in school, parents' night, my mother came. She was the most beautiful parent there, but she wore a man's coat and I wanted her to take it off. She wouldn't. At the display table, she read most of our Halloween booklets, each filled with poems and paragraph-long stories. When she came to mine, she read it, too, although she had already done so at home.

"Yours is the best," she said.

She talked to the teacher a long time, even when the teacher was trying to move away, anxiously nodding at other parents. I tugged at my mother's hand a little. Not much. She shook her head no and I retreated. But I heard.

"Could you give me a list of books he should read?"

"It's too soon for that. Junior high, five years from now, they have a reading list and. . . ."

"Can I get that? Can I get a copy of the list now?"

"I don't have one. Well, not in my room. I'm certain the principal. . . ."

My mother found the principal and came out of his office a short time later with a folder of papers.

Mrs. Sutton was waiting for us outside, in her car. She was half asleep.

"Arthur's the brightest one in that school," my mother said.

"Of course he is," Mrs. Sutton said.

"I mean it. A lot smarter than any of them."

All the way home, my mother tapped the knuckles of her right hand against the car window. Mrs. Sutton kept glancing that way. I was nervous, too, but it didn't matter. My mother thought I was the brightest person in the world.

She wanted to *help* me.

━

She began ordering books through the mail. She stacked them in my room and in the closet. She read a few. "I don't like them," she said. "But you read them. You need to know more than I do. Need to understand things, keep 'em where they're supposed to be."

Once she sat me down in the living room. She got on her knees in front of me and made me place my hands on her head. "I'm sorry if I offended you. Forgive me." She said it over and over.

"I forgive you," I said. Then she stood up. "You need a different mother, Arthur. You need somebody normal."

"I don't want a different mother."

She twisted her hands. "Oh, baby. I just don't want to be by myself. I do okay most of the time, don't I? Don't I take care of you?"

"You're a good mother." I clasped her knees. I was afraid she was going to give me away.

"I never beat you or anything. I feed you. I take care of you."

"I love you."

"You run over to Mrs. Sutton's for a while, okay?"

I ran. Mrs. Sutton was at her kiln, her dog swishing all happy to see me. I swept up the shop for her. She let me paint eyes on one of the ceramic squirrels. I was told to use blue and I did, but squirrels don't have blue eyes. I wanted to wipe the eyes off while they were wet, because they looked alive.

Mrs. Sutton fixed supper and said, "I'll check on your mom."

"No," I told her. "Let her alone."

She didn't go. I doubt if she really wanted to. We watched television and the dog lay beside me on the sofa. It was black and white and always in a frenzy. I soothed it with long strokes. Then I went to the little bedroom I always used at the Suttons. It had two windows and the lace curtains were never drawn. I lay awake part of the time, expecting to see my mother's face appear at the window. I did want her to come and I didn't.

I didn't want Mrs. Sutton to be my mother. She wasn't as pretty as my mother and she was dull. At that house, I felt truly imprisoned. Maybe it was because I would eventually go home. She helped keep me between lives, as if I floated somewhere along the road, looking for a place to be.

Mrs. Sutton would leave food in our refrigerator or on the counter, especially during those times when my mother might forget herself and me and the normal needs of a person had no place in her life. I might find a covered dish of potatoes or a roast or hamburger patties, something substantial. She asked me one afternoon if I liked onions and when I said, "No," she stopped putting them with our food. I had eaten them anyway, like them or not. She would occasionally bring a plate of them, all oily, having been cooked with meat. My mother liked them.

CHAPTER 7

MASON

Grace asked that I pick her up at 6:00 p.m. for our drive to Kansas City, and I did so but had to wait on her sofa while she finished dressing. She chatted toward me from the backrooms—bedroom and bathroom, I supposed—and once strolled into the living room, fully dressed but brushing her hair.

"So I'll drive. Is that all right? I know where we're going, and it will be less stress all the way around."

"Whatever makes you comfortable."

"It's only fair," she said. "After all, I invited you."

She retreated to the backrooms again, still chattering. I thought she had wanted me to admire the thickness and texture of her hair, that it was free of any artificial lift or control. It was also an intimate gesture, an act misplaced before a new guest in a living room. I knew she would soon take a bit of food from my plate or a piece of lint from my clothing. Women often gain territory in minute increments, because that method of aggression attracts least notice and is well tolerated. They're the weaker sex, and have to be careful how they gain and maintain any power at all. It's understandable.

We didn't leave for another quarter of an hour. I familiarized myself with her living room. She had good taste. The furnishings were expensive and understated, neutral colors and straight lines, but more for comfort than eye. The sofa and chairs were fully upholstered, no bare wood. A woman as small as she could curl up and sleep while watching television. The floor was hardwood, highshine, with a round, thick, red rug warming the conversation area. Small brass pieces and glass figurines were on the mantel, but the coffee table held only a huge ashtray, oversized books on various cities and countries, and a few atlases.

"I like to travel," she said, appearing as I leafed through one of the atlases. She wore a different outfit now, a black slim skirt long enough to brush her tiny ankles, and a red silk blouse. "Do you?"

"No, but I do it."

"Why, if you don't like to?" She had found keys and cigarettes and was ready at the door.

"In search of a career. Why else?"

"Poor man," she laughed. She had liked my response.

Grace didn't speed, but she darted in traffic as she darted in conversation, and would begin pulling into the next lane at the exact time she checked over her shoulder. It was a minute risk that was likely natural to her, and totally unconscious. At the restaurant, she cajoled our young server into giving his personal opinion of each entree. While Grace listened, his eyes noted all the tables he wasn't at, all the tips winking away during his dutiful obeisance to the lovely diner at my table.

But she *was* beautiful, fine-tuned, sharply gracious. I recognized her human loneliness and I pitied her a little. Perhaps she didn't know that she demeaned herself by flirting with waiters and doormen and demeaned them, too. Suppose they found her repulsive and were forced, by their position, to treat her not only with courtesy but with feigned attraction and even fondness?

"So," she said that evening, after sharing some of her history, "there you have it. My personal, trivial drama. He left me for a student, and now they have a house in Palm Beach, one in Vegas, and one in Mexico City."

"You've done well enough yourself."

"Mason, Missouri?" Her contempt was evident.

"You have a Ph.D., a permanent job. Respect. I would be happy to stay here. I hope I have the chance."

"Oh," she said. "Sorry. I wasn't thinking that staying here might actually be a goal."

She was, I think, genuinely, though briefly, embarrassed, and she should have been.

She herself didn't seem to respect much other than correct social behavior. She called students "little twits." She said Nada was a "born servant."

"I'm serious," she said. "Nada longs for a swift boot to the rear end. She wants to be the king's chambermaid, the mayor's kitchen girl."

"You shouldn't talk about people like that."

"I didn't say *we* wanted her to be a servant. I said she's a born servant. She would have done well in another age, when a good servant was appreciated."

"But you think she should keep her place."

"Well, yes. You'll know what I mean after a while."

I did know what she meant and wasn't in total disagreement. Nada deserved an appropriate niche. Those who are successful in life have an obligation to others, to provide them with the dignity of self-support, of good performance, and of adequate reward. Mockery has no place in the exchange.

The discussion reminded me of a woman I once knew, and I wanted to tell Grace so. Sometimes I get these urges to warn women—to tell them it's a dark night and they're nearing a precipice blindly. I did it as best I could, given the situation. If I believed in mistakes, that would have been one.

"You remind me of a teacher I had."

"Is this good or bad?"

"Neither. Just a reminder."

"Tell me. Tell me the story. What's her name?"

"Juliette. Juliette Preston."

"Nice name. Now. The tale of Juliette Preston."

"She liked people to obey rules. There was a kid in class, a country bumpkin. Like Charles Bovary, you know? Couldn't learn. But he was so happy to be at a university. She failed everything he wrote. I offered to help him. I didn't write the paper, but I gave him hints and I personally corrected his errors. I checked his final draft. Not a mechanical flaw in it."

"And what did she do?"

"The kid blurted out in class, 'Why'd I get an F? You don't say why.' She replied, 'Because it's vacuous.'"

Grace leaned forward. "I bet I know what comes next—the boy said, 'What's vacuous?'"

"Right."

Grace laughed, delighted. "They're precious. Stupid and precious." Moments later, she said, "It wasn't you, was it? That Charles Bovary kid?"

"Of course not."

"I couldn't imagine he was you. You're obviously bright."

"Moderately so."

"Nice response." She sipped a little wine, lowered the glass, but continued to hold it. She was focused on me. "You have a wonderful voice. I'm sure you've been told that. It's very mellow, rich, and soft. You'd make a good announcer."

I've been told that I have a soothing voice, but I've never liked public speaking—so many listeners and expectations. I prefer quiet, even silence. Of course, I can converse spontaneously and well in most situations. "Maybe it helps me be a decent teacher," I said.

She was a good conversationalist once she slowed into talk instead of performance. She was well-read, fond of movies, and well-versed in current events. She considered the latter inappropriate for dinner conversations. I came to movies late, but have learned to like them. Our common ground was love of literature. "Have you read" was an acceptable exchange between us.

⌒

The Charles Bovary kid was named Stephen Dunham. He dropped out of school. He was a nice young man about my own age, with pretty shabby clothes and a rather natural shabbiness all about him. He couldn't help that, I imagine.

⌒

"You're jittery, aren't you?" Grace said that evening.

"No. I just felt sorry for our waiter."

"Don't. He gets good tips."

There was little traffic back to Mason. The night sky was a blue-black flatness, a few stars visible if one searched. Grace kept me engaged in conversation, though it wasn't necessary. The evening was enjoyable. As we neared the town, she became a little agitated, as if she were driving into the reality of her own situation.

"I guess you're going to be Nada's new champion," she said.

"Well, she needs one, if anybody does. But she'll unseat you. You wait and see. We've all tried, and the only way to help Nada is in secret, anonymously. Else her gratitude will kill you."

At her house, a yard light had come on, that false amber shine that is bright at the pole but dims in the reaches where it's really needed. And the windows were alight. She had either turned lamps on before we left or had them timed to switch on.

"Would you like some coffee or a drink?" she asked.

"I've had too much of both, but I'll come in if you like."

"Would you? Just long enough for me to take a look around."

Then I understood why she appeared ill at ease. The woman didn't like nighttime, at least nighttime alone. She wanted to hold it back by bright conversation and by the sheer will to continue daytime.

She fumbled open the door and I came just inside. I didn't settle down. I left the door open behind me and waited. Her chatter wove around as she poked her head into all the rooms.

"All's well," she said, coming into the living room. "Aren't you going to sit down?"

"If you don't mind, I'll go on home now. I've had a hard week and still have things to unpack. Especially books."

"All right. Fine. Well," she came up to me, her left hand reaching for the door. It's a moment when a woman may turn one way or another to indicate the door will close you in or out.

"I had a very good time," she said.

"So did I. You've been very gracious to me. Everyone has."

She followed me to the stoop and down the steps, her arms crossed over her midriff, hands cupping her elbows. "I have high hopes," she said gaily, "that you'll spark up this little town. It could use some creative force. At dinner parties alone."

By the yard lamp, I stopped walking. She wasn't ready for me to go.

"Would you like me to come back in?" I asked. "Do you want me to check out the basement? I noticed you didn't do that."

"Oh, no. No." She shook her head and waved that idea away. "I'm just wired from the coffee and the evening. The basement's no bother. There's no door and the windows are small. I keep the inside door locked when I'm gone."

She was at the edge of the light, her dress and shoes visible but her face hidden. "I redid this whole front yard this summer," she said. "Or, rather, I *had* it done. Brick retaining walls for the flower beds, and juniper bushes everywhere. They'll stay green all winter, even in snow, and I like that. People in Mason don't care much about beauty. You've probably noticed that?"

"I've rented a nice place."

"Where?"

"Claxston Arms."

"Really? They rent to students, don't they?"

"Yes, they do."

"Well you couldn't pay me to stay there. We see little student bodies all week. I wouldn't want to know more about them than I do now." Her hands worried at the hem of her blouse. She couldn't let our evening come to an end. "I'd probably do better in an apartment," she said. "One in Paris, especially."

After a short silence, I said, "Good night, then?"

"Yes, good night, sir gentleman."

She turned back to the house and I waited till she was at the door, giving me a tiny wave. When it closed, I went on down the drive to the street and my car. Her basement windows were dark.

I've read that women who wish to be safe should pay close attention to details around their home. They should leave lights on and if one of those lights is not on when they return, they should call for a friend to enter with them. A porch light is especially crucial. It can so easily be unscrewed just enough to go black. A person can enter the top of a house and go down into the basement and then back up. So Grace was allowing herself the safety only of routine. I thought I would one day tell her that, if she was open to suggestions.

We became lovers a week later. She was straightforward about wanting intimacy. We were looking through an art book together, seated on her beige sofa, by a lamp that cast light upward, like a flat ghost moon on the ceiling. Soft lighting is important to women. I remember a scene in which an actor forces an older woman up against a wall and rips the cover from a Japanese lantern. Her age is exposed. He knew what she looked like before he did that. He just wants her to know what he knows. His act was deep, deliberate cruelty. It's the revealing of ugliness that makes it unbearable, not the simple state of it.

Grace closed the book and said, "Should we see how compatible we are?" That was explicit enough.

"If you like."

"Don't hedge," she said. "I want to know what *you* like."

"Let's see how compatible we are," I echoed, and she chuckled, as she often did, low key, nothing raucous.

She said, "I'll meet you in the bedroom."

That allowed me to use the restroom, allowed her to prepare herself. She was very orderly in her approach, even to pleasures.

She stood right beside the bed, wearing a filmy black thing that didn't suit her sharpness, but maybe it was for only an immediate effect, because she slipped it from her shoulders and stepped free. Her little body was exquisite, far finer than it appeared in clothing. That may have given her some of her confidence. She had pulled the covers of the bed back, to the very bottom, and had lit two candles. They were unscented, though I could smell their heat.

She enjoyed sex. I do, too, but I don't talk about it needlessly or in any crude way.

"I knew you were a good one," Grace whispered. "But be discreet, okay? Especially at the office. I don't like everyone to know my business."

"I don't tell any secrets," I assured her. "Not mine or any one else's."

I wasn't at all secure with having such a relationship at my place of work. Now my attention would be divided and I would have to meet a wider range of expectations. But I had no choice.

⟼

I saw a weaver bird once who couldn't get his nest right. He struggled, pulling the grass and straw into intricate patterns. He occasionally fell in his frenzy. And when he finished, he sat on the nest chirping for a female to inspect it. None came. Not one. He chirped his fat little body into thinness. Then, as that species does, he ripped the nest apart and started all over again.

⟼

Juliette Preston. Just after *Fathers* was published, I was driving through Tennessee. On the roadside ahead a huge billboard had been partially stripped of its former message and now proclaimed in massive block letters: "YOUR SPACE HERE." As I drew closer, bits of the original message were readable, something about "Guardians of the Future." It caused me to remember Miss Preston. She wasn't a pretty woman, which may have been part of her problem. She had a slit mouth and hog eyes. I recalled that she had found a teaching position in Glenville, somewhere in Tennessee. I looked it up on the map. It was only one hundred and fifty miles out of my way. I spent two nights in a motel on the outskirts of the town, found a J. Preston in the phonebook, and telephoned her from a convenience store about 7:00 a.m. on Saturday morning. I reminded her that I had once been her student and explained that my book was being published. She was pleased; she hoped she had been partly responsible for my success.

"Are you living here now?" she asked.

"No, just passing through."

"That's too bad. I'd like to see you."

"Have breakfast with me," I said. "We can toast both our accomplishments."

I picked her up. If she had had a husband or roommate, the day would have been different. But she lived alone. She was immediately ready. She brought a camera along, but I asked her to wait for pictures until we had eaten. She became alarmed when we exited the highway.

"Where are we going?" she said. When I didn't answer, her voice became demanding. "You stop this car. You stop it now."

I didn't obey immediately.

During the following hours, I took pictures of her. I left the camera, film inside, in another state two years later.

She was an unkind person.

I don't know why I took pictures. Photographs have been important to me at different times, but not those, and I never took pictures again. She brought the camera.

⟵

See? I'm not hiding anything here. I try not to think about these incidents, but sometimes something brings them to mind, as I might be reminded about a book I read or a movie I saw. Grace had reminded me.

⟵

Nada, of all people, had read *Fathers*. "I got it through library loan," she said, "the minute I knew you were hired." She thought, she said, she'd like more description, "more feeling." But she assured me that she was "nobody to judge," and besides, "the critics liked it." She quoted a few. "They called it a 'stark journey into melancholia,' a 'moving restraint of pain.'"

"I'm indebted to you for caring enough to read it."

"And I liked it."

"Yes, and especially for liking it."

"I write, too, you know. I'm going to take your class next semester."

"Good. I'll be glad to have you."

She was happy, so easily made happy. At the door, she turned and blurted, "Dr. Burch likes men, you know. She counts them up and brags sometimes. Just to us girls, though."

Nada did talk too much, as others have said, but she was a master of brevity as well.

Of course, Grace liked men. Even waiters knew that. But Nada wanted to warn me and that was an admirable motive.

⤙

I didn't pursue Nada herself in any way, not even by stepping inside her office. I saw it, since the door was usually open. It was a shameful assignment, at best. She shared it with other assistants or adjuncts. Their desks were aligned along the west wall, the only marker of territory a trashcan between each desk. Nada's space was on the opposite wall, at the end, in a wedge corner by the window. But the corner blazoned old calendar pictures, greeting cards, magazine covers, and the like. A filing cabinet at the nearer end of the desk provided a semblance of cubicle. Atop it was a large round vase of roses. They overflowed the vase, drooped curving over the glass as if wilting. They had to be false, and when I passed the door another time and saw them in the same condition, I knew they were.

Harper saw me looking in the second time. "Going in or coming out?"

"Passing by."

"Wise," he said.

I had to admire Nada again. The department gave her half a tunnel and she made it a miniature parlor. Resilient, resourceful old gal.

CHAPTER 8

GEORGIA, 1951

I was ten when I accepted responsibility for my own care. I woke late one morning. It was still black outside. I struggled into my school clothes and ran downstairs, worried by something I sensed. Maybe the house was too quiet. Maybe she'd made a noise. She was nowhere. There was no breakfast on the table or stove. A piece of paper was at my place. "You want to eat? Then cook." I found another note on the stove. "Wipe up after yourself." Throughout the house there were notes: "Dry the sink." "Dust this." "Mop this."

I had to catch the school bus. I got my coat and went outside. She was standing at the edge of the yard, where the gravel road to the main road began. She wore one of the long coats from the closet but she was barefoot. That scared me.

"You clean up?"

"I washed my dishes."

"I said, did you clean up?"

"Yes."

"Did you clean up everything?"

"I got to get to school."

"No you don't. I let you go to school. That's my doing."

I took one step toward the road and she took one step as if to block me.

"I don't like school anyway," I said.

"The whole house is filthy. Everything's running rot."

I went back in. I stayed home the rest of the week. The school called. She told them we had both been sick. She stopped paying attention to what I did. As long as I kept moving around, she left me alone. When I fell asleep finally, on the living room floor, she woke me up and led me to the bathroom. She stripped me, stood me in the tub. She got the scrub brush from the kitchen and scraped me raw all over. I cried a little. Then she stood in the tub and scrubbed herself.

These events weren't pleasant, I agree. But they occurred infrequently, over a long period of time. In between, she was often a plainer woman, with her hair pulled back or loose and falling in nice shapes across her cheek or neck. She would then fall to work, cleaning house, cupboards, drawers, calling the store for groceries. Calling me. "Arthur!" "Arthur!" "Arthur! Come eat dinner!"

She never struck me. She did absolutely the best she could. How could anybody quarrel with that? Or claim otherwise?

And there was Mrs. Sutton, to piecemeal my care. Steadily, steadily, to watch Arthur grow.

I gradually learned to prepare food and found groceries in the kitchen as often or more often than prepared dishes. And as a result, I can take care of myself. I know all the female arts, cooking, cleaning, sewing. Even nurturing.

CHAPTER 9

MASON

The animal kingdom teaches us a lot about the human situation. Maybe that's why I've been fascinated all my life with the actions of other species. We evolved side by side, at the very least, under the same dome of heaven, ran along the same grids, escaped, died. In many species, the males are often kicked out, run off by the females. True loners may pair up, not from loneliness, but for attack. Brutes together.

But a *social* creature forced to live separate may go berserk. If the loner is patient, subservient, hangs around the edges of a gathering, the others get accustomed to him, sniff him out, let him in closer and closer, stroke him in. He's one of us, now, no threat. If he wants in the group, his own nature can't matter much. He has to give it up. He has to become not what *he's* drawn to, but what's drawn to *him*.

⟶

Grace liked to play Botticelli, a deceptively simple guessing game. One person thinks of a literary figure—if that's the category—offers the others only the beginning letter of the figure's last name, then defends the secret by answering questions. But there's a complexity in the questions: The poser knows the answer and must give valid, fair clues in the question and still mislead the defender. I listened to her and others in the lounge until I was certain of the rules. When she was restless one evening, at her place, I suggested a game.

"You've learned it! Have you played yet? With Harper or somebody?"

"I've just been listening to all of you. Go ahead. Start."

"Okay. Good." She was wearing red pajamas, sitting cross-legged on the floor with her lecture notes before her. She scooted up to the table, lit a cigarette, and said "S. The name begins with S."

I composed my first attempt to stump her. "Did you write of a girl, mercy, and a strainer?"

"What?"

I repeated it.

"Oh, Arthur. That's awful. No, I'm not Shakespeare."

"Shakespeare what? Which work?"

"I guessed who you meant. That's enough."

"No. You have to identify the work, too. Otherwise, it could be a wild stab. I've been paying attention. You always have to name the work."

"You're right. I wasn't thinking. Okay. My response should have been '*Merchant of Venice*. No, I'm not Shakespeare.' Sorry."

"Thank you."

"Next one, please," she said.

"All right. Cans in a row."

She frowned, looked down in thought. It was a nice image. "Cans in a row. Cans in a row." She looked at me. "That can't be a legitimate clue. It's too scant."

"It's more than sufficient."

She continued worrying at it.

"Have I stumped you?"

"Not yet."

"We should put a time limit on responding."

She raised her hands. "Okay. But that isn't a decent clue."

"I'll give you another, just to be fair."

"I accept. What is it?"

"Bipeds and rodents."

"Idiot! What kind of clue is that? You're not . . . oh, wait a minute." Her eyebrows raised, recognition lighted her eyes. "I know," she said. "*Of Mice and Men*. It's Steinbeck. And the other, the other is. . . . Damn. What is that work. Yeah. *Cannery Row*."

"Exactly," I said.

"I love this game," she said. "You'll have to join us in the lounge."

"No," I said. "I just wanted you to know I could do it."

"You had me stumped. You would have earned a clue."

"That's all right. I don't mind."

She was thrilled with me. She kissed me, put away her lecture notes, and came to sit by me. We watched a movie together.

"You like the way I play?" I asked her later.

"You know I do."

I liked her, especially her determination to make the best of every moment, to be as happy as she could manage.

⟶

By a bit of good luck, I won a small handmade bird for Grace. A group of us at the department had agreed to attend Mason's fall street fair, and though Grace and I couldn't go together, we agreed where and when to run into each other. When I arrived, she was standing on the sidewalk eating something from a small Styrofoam container.

"That's not like you," I said.

"I'm glad you know that," she said. "It's chili. I have a weakness for spicy foods, even peasant food."

The others came along soon enough to keep us from appearing a couple, and we strolled down the street, not stopping at any of the craft or club booths, observers only. When we reached the gaming stalls, Loeffle wanted to play and urged Walsh and me to join him. We begged off for the same reason—we were no good at these things. Neither was Loeffle, but in good spirit he spent ten or more dollars to win his wife an odd-shaped bear suitable for a small child. But she liked it. She held it up for Grace and Mrs. Walsh to admire. "Would you like one?" I asked Grace, which was foolish. She said "No" and we all walked on. But I had awakened a possibility. I saw it in Grace's glances. She didn't want the object itself, the bear, but she wanted *something*. They always do. So at the dart booth, I bought my five tries. I had no expectations of hitting the target, and thought the draft of the weapon probably displaced the object. But I felt compelled to try.

My first toss, my first flip of the wrist at the yellow balloon and it popped as if it were meant to, had perhaps burst before the dart hit. Walsh or Loeffle whooped, and one said, "Way to go." The women applauded.

A slip of paper floated down and the booth man picked it up. "Number twelve," he said. "That's the birds. Take your choice."

They didn't look real, but they were fairly well done, with real feathers, glass eyes, and black feet, the latter made of some heavy, flexible plastic. Grace gave me no sign, so I chose the yellow one. I offered it to her.

"Well, thank you," she said, looking at the others. "Are you sure you don't want it?"

"I'm absolutely certain," I said. "But don't feel obligated to take it."

"No. I think it's cute. And I appreciate the gesture. Thank you." She met my eyes that time. A risk, I suppose.

She put it in her dining room window.

"That's the first time anyone ever championed *me*," she said.

"Why don't you put it in the bedroom?"

"Nope. Birds carry tales."

We both laughed.

It seemed a wonderfully good omen.

‒

Grace would not go to department social functions with me. "If people think we're a couple, and then we break up," she said, "they'll believe you dumped me."

"Why? Why not believe the reverse?"

"Because I'm an older woman and you're a man. That's what people would believe. I don't make the rules, Arthur, but I know them and following them makes life easier."

So I assumed she had had affairs with colleagues. That was her prerogative, and didn't matter to me, though it meant someone might be observing us who knew what was occurring, who could read the signs. She was witty and kept the surface of any interaction glittering. Even in meetings, she quipped often, authority be damned. But she had no *real* power over tenured personnel, so they must have found her miniature outbursts simply diverting.

Grace's affection for me, pretended or real, was puzzling. "Why do you like me?" I asked.

"You've the air of a gentleman," she said, "and you dress well. You have a real sense of style, at least old-world style. You put these Mason men to shame. They confuse promptness with graciousness and tipping with generosity. After living here a while, it's easy to get sloppy, in dress and attitudes."

"So they're beneath you?"

"No. Well, in some ways maybe they are. Too many of them rest on their laurels. They like to wield power and make everyone over-achieve to meet criteria they invented but never had to meet." She came to sit on my lap, which never failed to startle me. She would be talking from one nature and acting another. "Now you," she nuzzled my cheek, "are going to withstand their peculiar torture. I'm going to help you."

She was up again, without slipping into intimacy from sheer proximity. She controlled it, like an evening out or a conversation. Her skin was the most beautiful texture. I wanted to trace the lines of her cheeks and collarbones and tiny ribcage, and sometimes I did. She could be very quiet then, though normally she was a constant sound.

Now, she said, "Of course, your main appeal is that you're male, totally, totally male."

"Prime requisite?"

"Absolutely."

That, of course, was true, without my having any say.

—

Grace would have liked for me to slip into her house in the dark hours, stay until she fell asleep, and leave before dawn. She didn't say so, but I knew. She feared being alone, especially at night. When I made motions toward leaving, she had a repertoire of phrases and fetching looks. "Oh, so soon?" "Surely there's something we could do?" "I have a wonderful old movie." "Did I tell you what Dr. Walsh said about the pay increase?" "Let's read a play together, Arthur. You choose the play." "Wait until I've taken a bath, will you? I'm afraid to take a bath when I'm alone in the house."

It wasn't a lover's voice she used. I don't know what kind of voice it was, but it was very appealing. And I usually stayed for a little while, especially when she bathed. She left the door open, and the moist heat gradually came to the living room, like a path to her.

⟶

On two of our excursions into the city, she had me pick her up in a small town along the highway. Lone Jack. She thought the name was very funny. Once, when we inadvertently sat side by side in a meeting, she wrote "Lone Jack" on her tablet where I could see. So could others. It had no meaning isolated like that, but it was a game she played. Catch me.

She outranked me. And she always would, unless they failed to promote her to the last step. I was an assistant professor, but temporary, which made the title meaningless to all but students. In rank, I was really no more than an adjunct, an instructor. Grace was an associate professor and could at any time apply for full professorship. "I'm going to apply," she said, "as soon as I feel that my record is strong enough to fight for myself, because I will probably have to appeal. I don't want to give any old boy a weapon from my own arsenal."

She liked used and rare bookstores and ferreted around in them. In one, she tripped down narrow, spiraling stairs to a tiny, round room and soon squealed, "Arthur! I've found a most wonderful book!"

So I went down, too. The air was thick and dusty, and the stacks so close, so cramped, that we couldn't move without brushing against books. We were like rats in a corn bin.

"James's *Turn of the Screw*," she said. "Isn't that one of your favorites?"

She knew it was.

She leafed through a few pages. "Look at these illustrations. It's the Flower and Hand Edition, London 1940. I can't believe it, stuck on a shelf down here. I'll get it for you."

She was a picture herself, bow mouth parted, black eyes shining. I kissed her. She trembled a little. When I drew away and attempted to take the book, she clutched it to her breast. "Now I must have it," she said. "To remember this moment."

Her feelings for me had altered in some way. I assumed her statement was a compliment, but the entire exchange was a contradiction.

Grace was very physical and wanted that trait simultaneously revealed and concealed. She was far more a creature of pleasures than even I had guessed.

The creative writing classes were assigned a basement classroom. It had one half-window near the ceiling, giving only to an unused walk at the back of building; damp, flaking walls; an overhead light too dim for the size of the room. Pallid in such light, the students seated at the large seminar table looked like hungry little cadavers.

Why should the kids respect me? How could I make them feel their writing had value when the department relegated all of us to leftover, ugly space and to late afternoon or evening hours? People believe writers like only dark places, that they indulge all vices, bloat the body with gluttony of the spirit. But these same writers are supposed to save enough of themselves to crawl out, to grab pen and paper, and to write sunbursts of hope for the rest of the world.

I was a good teacher. I enjoyed all those kids, though only three were talented: Jack Goff, whom I had spotted the first time I met him at my apartment building, Billy Butler, and Sarah Fulkerson. They grouped together within the first two weeks, leaning toward each other for praise, arguing with me when I advised them to write what they *couldn't*, to risk, reach. I quoted Browning: "'Ah, but a man's reach should exceed his grasp, or what's a heaven for.'"

"If Browning's work was being graded," Jack said, "he might have been more cautious."

A few students laughed. They were all attentive now.

"I doubt that. And you don't strike me as cautious, anyhow."

"I'm not cautious, but I'm not foolish either. Who wants to fail over and over? If that happened to me, I'd get out of the field and go into something else."

"You're misinterpreting the statement. It means to be in competition with yourself, to try to attain your highest goals."

He shook his head. "I haven't misinterpreted," he insisted. "We're saying the same thing, only you find it positive and I don't."

"Well, let's leave it at that, then, a gentlemen's disagreement."

He shrugged. "Okay."

I wish he had been able to like me.

Sarah, a rather generic girl, pretty, intelligent, but low-key, wanted Jack. I could spot her restrained, deep-felt desire. But he was being also pursued by one Justinia. The name should have clued me to her function, a woman who would bring a man to his basest level. She often waited for Jack outside the building, leaning voluptuously and deliberately against the concrete wall. I met her in the Union with Sarah one day. Justinia sat down, draped both arms over the back of the chair, effectively pointing her breasts at us. She was so filled with herself, the universe was a pea she could balance on the tip of her tongue.

"Come watch me dance sometime," she said, when Sarah had left for class. "I'm pretty good."

"I imagine you are."

"I've signed up to pose for Live Drawing students."

"Have you? Why would you do that?"

"Money," she said, which wasn't the only reason, if it mattered at all. She was so hungry.

I knew she was after me, too, though she didn't want to catch me in the way she wanted to catch Jack. She wanted me to run pell-mell and lusty after her, so she could stop me in my tracks. It's true I am sometimes drawn to sheer sensuality. Justinia, little unscrupulous twist, was wallowing in it.

Paul Harper happened to see us that day. Later he poked his head in my office long enough to slur, "Don't mess with Masonite munchkins. They bite." His language and movements always startled me. They were too slow and soft for his shape.

Harper was a brilliant man and possibly a good lecturer, but he thought most students were unworthy of space in his classroom. When the semester was underway, he waved a handful of pink slips at me.

"See these," he said. "Drop slips. My largest class is now down to fifteen students; my smallest, to six. Decent numbers. Now perhaps we can have an intellectual discussion."

I tried to keep students in my classes; he tried to boot his out. We weren't alike at all.

Harper vehemently disliked Mason. He left town most weekends, occasionally taking the train. Mason's depot, long closed and boarded up, sat at the bottom of Main Street, in the shadow of a looming grain mill. I saw Harper waiting there one Friday evening. He was dressed for rough walking—khaki slacks, hiking boots, dark green parka, and backpack. Army issue, though he had never been in the service. He never said why he wasn't chosen to fight for someone's freedom. He swayed slightly, forward and back, as he stared and waited. With his broad shoulders and the hump on his back, he looked like a cobra that rears up tall, much of its body coiling for the spring of strike. The railway guard lowered, stopping my car, and when it raised again, the depot was empty and Harper was gone.

"Where do you go when you leave Mason?" I later asked him.

"Libraries, mostly. Ours is a joke."

"In hiking gear?"

"Why not? I order it through army surplus catalogues. Their stuff goes for practically nothing."

"Were you in the military?"

"Heavens, no. I respect real soldiers, though, whether leaders or followers. You weren't in the service, were you, Arthur?"

"No."

"So we have that in common. What we haven't done."

"You don't actually hike at all?"

"Of course I do. I cruise the mountains of great minds, taking my little pickax to claim nuggets of truth." He wriggled a pen at me. "Besides, I have to go somewhere. I don't want to turn into a Masonite. Something creeps up on the denizens of this fair burg, turns them into small-minded, stultifying slugs. Or hadn't you noticed? See any socializing going on here? We don't even like each other."

Harper read the campus newsletters and knew who had published and where. He hadn't read any of Grace's papers, but he believed they had to be more than competent. "They're in good journals," he said, "and you can tell the woman's no lightweight."

He sometimes paused at my office door just to raise his brows. "Carry on," he would say.

Carry on what? I wondered then. Carry on what?

CHAPTER 10

GEORGIA, 1953

There was a little boy once, about twelve years old, who may have gone through a cruel phase. He caught a tree toad, one of those exceedingly small toads that looks like a knot of bark. He found it magical and charming for a few hours one afternoon. But when dinner time approached, he trapped the toad with a can, went in the house, and took a fork from a kitchen drawer. He took the fork outside, released the toad, then speared it. He watched it struggle for a while, then he carried the fork and toad to the backyard. A few feet from the steps to the porch, he stuck the fork handle into the soil. He left the little sign there for his mother to find. He thought about it while he and his mother had dinner.

The next morning, when she went outside, he stood at the kitchen window. She did see the fork and toad. She picked it up and turned to look at the window. He stayed where she could see him. She walked to the clothesline pole and wiped the fork against the wood. She brought the fork back in the house and placed it where he usually sat at the table. He stayed in the house all day, but she never left it either. Even when she went to the bathroom, she left the door open. He ate lunch and dinner with his fingers.

"Use the fork, Arthur," she said.

"No."

"Use it. I don't do mean things deliberately unless there's a good purpose."

He still ate with his fingers. Then he took the fork into the woods and buried it.

When he killed other small creatures, he didn't bring them home. He left them for her to encounter on her walks.

He tried to castrate the Sutton dog with a pocket knife, but all he succeeded in doing was injuring the animal, which yelped, slunk, and then ran away, and then would not sit near the boy at the Sutton house. When the dog died of cancer a few years later, the boy missed it.

The cruel phase, if it occurred at all, was brief, a little over a year. He was never certain if he actually did those things or only thought about them.

⌒

Academically, I succeeded. Teachers always encouraged me to "go on with my schooling." "Think about college." "Try for scholarships." I liked school, that's for sure. I'd do anything to get that little bit of praise. I imagine I was pathetic.

The girls liked me for conversation. One of them had freckles and was tall and bony and was sometimes teased about her thin shanks. She endured it good-naturedly. She had blue eyes with black fringe eyelashes. She would look directly at me and smile, without saying anything. She may have liked me.

I wonder, how does a female like that grow up to be? Can she stay so calm and accepting?

The real oddball in our school was a kid who couldn't keep his hands out of his pockets. He played with himself from junior high through high school. Walter Trenton. He was slack-mouthed, slope-eyed, and disgusting. Teachers tried, at first, sending him from the room, to counselors. I suppose they contacted his parents. But nature persisted, and Walter embarrassed us all from time to time, just caught in his own fantasy. Amazingly, he passed every course. No. Perhaps it isn't amazing. I would have promoted him, too. Who would keep him two years?

"I'll try, Arthur," my mother said, "to put by some money for college. You just make the grades."

She probably intended to try, but the idea of money became corrupted by whatever boiled in her. Years later, in one of her flights of fancy, she did something with it all. I think I know what.

⟶

Poor Walter Trenton. He didn't know what behavior to hide.

CHAPTER 11

MASON

When Justinia and I ran into each other, she would make some incongruous movement that sometimes tripped a sound from me. Once she cupped the underside of her breasts, lifting them like gifts. I don't like crudity, but she twisted it into playfulness.

If I was alone, she always greeted me with, "Hi, Bloomin' Arthur."

I did watch her dance, but not at the Club, where, she said, she displayed her body and rhythm around a pole, or near a customer's table, or on his lap. I went into Boogy's and had wine and watched the students dance together. I liked the duality of it, the attempt to bridge differences toward a mutual pleasure. Justinia asked me to dance and I said "No." So she danced with some square-headed boy with slim hips and a one-step dance. She looked at me over his shoulder, which wasn't fair to the poor fellow. It was furtive unkindness. He had earned his time of her total attention, worthless as it might have been.

She invited me to a party at her apartment, and I wasn't blind to her motives. She wanted to display me, position me here and there to please her vanity. I was glad to go, though, because students need to know that professors are accessible and that they value student life. To put oneself above them is to create little monsters, because they *will* follow suit. They will harbor resentment, aspire to a higher place themselves, and then abuse it. Many of them, at least. Perhaps not Sarah. She seemed not to be a threat to anyone, capable of feeling passion but not of pursuing it or even inspiring it. Anyone would be safe with her.

But, to the party: Many, many young people, not in the least awed by me—I had already been claimed.

"Are you the writer? Justinia said you were coming."

"I'm the very person you speak of, but that's not much to say."

"She says you're famous."

"No." I raised a finger. "I have one book."

"That's more than I got." He shook my hand and wandered off, pants falling down, beer firmly gripped.

The place was smoky and the walls thrummed a musical noise.

Justinia snaked her way to me, wearing some kind of half top and half skirt, so her torso was in three. Her belly button was adorned with a gold stud. I find that application of the word "stud" humorous, though apt.

"Hi, Bloomin' Arthur."

"Hello yourself."

"I didn't think you'd come."

"Why not? You invited me."

"You're sort of an old fuddy-duddy."

"That doesn't sound like you. What do you really call me?"

She whispered a mild obscenity that didn't become her but did make me laugh.

"I told people about you," she said. "Did you bring your book with you?"

"No, I didn't. That's not the way it's done in academic circles."

"It would be in my circle. Where I went, it would go. 'Hey, hey,' I'd say, 'meet *my* product.'"

"You are a product. A remarkable one."

"Want to see it all?"

"Some other time."

"For sure?"

"For sure."

I stayed long enough to prove the party enjoyable and myself available and compliant. When I went outside, the air had chilled. Some moments alone are so precious, so rare and delicious, one's whole body tastes them.

In the art gallery, most of the sketches and paintings of Justinia were prophetic. She was distorted, disproportionate, shaped by un-trained and some unskilled hands. But Jack Goff, whose work was displayed on another wall, had given her better treatment in a small oil. She was curled, shoulders in as if the breasts were too heavy. Her left hand rested flat on her lower stomach, the outer curve of palm against the pubic line, suggesting both exposure and conceal-ment, or the moment of decision. The colors were gentle, rosy, and pale yellow and light blue.

I assumed Justinia would be flattered. But she said, when I men-tioned it, "Jack doesn't like what I'm doing. He looks at me but he doesn't see me."

"I think he sees you quite well."

"No. He sees me better than I am."

She wasn't quite as empty-headed as I had thought.

Go figure, as the kids today say. That's a nice, tight little phrase, implying mathematical thought combined with physical action.

⟶

Nada thought I was fine, absolutely fine. And I thought the same of her. If she was pathetic, she was also admirable. She was just an old lady, peeking around the margins, trying to find entry and acceptance. She talked too much. She bustled one to death. But she *worked*. She worked every minute of every day: run to the library, make the coffee, wash the cups, copy the exams, type up the notes, clear the bulletin board, get doughnuts for the meeting. She took classes, and when she wasn't scurrying on an errand for someone, she was in her little corner, reading, taking notes, writing her own papers. She swirled like powder around all of us.

My colleagues encouraged her labors, paid her a pittance, and called it charity. They didn't even have the grace to respect her. They ridiculed her. Harper would mimic her even when she was in the same room, her back turned. He would mince up his face, duck his head, raise his hand as if to ward off a blow. The skeleton joker.

If Nada knew, she never let on. She was wise.

I came back to campus late one evening and found her asleep in the lounge, her fleshy, pale arms wrapped around a stack of papers she was using for a pillow. Other stacks formed a semicircle on the table. I read the names of the teachers. Five professors. She was grading papers for *five* professors.

I was ashamed of them all.

⟶

"She *wants* to grade for me," Grace said. "She pestered me until I gave her a set of essays to grade. Why can't you see that we let Nada do those things because she wants to? We don't even want her around, the sneaky old woman. She cleans the lounge because it gets her inside, where she can listen and feel important. She wants power, Arthur. She's attached herself to you just in case you're a valuable asset. Don't underestimate her."

"I guess that means we're allowed to abuse if the victim requests it. That's an easy way out of responsibility."

"If anyone's a victim here, it's us. We don't even want the old bat here. Don't you know she's what everyone is afraid of becoming?"

We were in Grace's office for this discussion, with the door wide open. She held court there, unless students came by. But for colleagues, she kept a bowl of candy, kept herself cheerful and unoccupied, ready for their brief company.

Her office displayed Nada's touch, too—a stuffed bear sat on the computer, a wire from his collar holding aloft a dialog box: "Any minute, I'm going to screen."

"You like the bear," she said. "You always smile when you look at it."

"Do I? It's the play on words."

"I know," she said. "You like words. You should. You're a writer." She glanced toward the door. "But there's one word I'd like to hear you say, especially in a whisper."

"And what's that?" I thought it would be an endearment or the crucial "love."

"Grace," she whispered. "My own personal appellation." She put her finger to her lips as if that's where I might say the word.

She was an observer, too, with her own perspective, and with a penchant for speaking it.

⟶

I'm not a brave man, and being new to the circle I was in a tenuous position, but I tried to help Nada. I spoke about her with the dean and the department chair.

"Everyone takes advantage of her," I told the dean. "Even if she asks for it, they shouldn't pile work on her. They should protect her from herself."

"She pretty much selects her own duties. That's the only way to keep her bearable."

"She can't," the chair said, "see a scrap out of place, or let a phone ring, or hear a question without answering. She's invaded everyone's space and privacy. And, unfortunately, she has alienated Margaret to the point that we've had to ask Nada not to step behind the counter, even to use the phone. Margaret says Nada has managed to get a key to the main office and goes through the files. I feel sorry for Nada, too. Most of us do. But we'd still like to get rid of her, and she makes it difficult."

She had created some fiasco with interlibrary loans. She had written the president and Board of Regents about insufficient copy paper, inadequate ventilation, and rough paper towels. She had carried a space heater into a cold classroom and tripped the switch for an entire wing. She entered empty offices uninvited, to open blinds or dust knickknacks.

I tried to get her a mailbox, but even that they wouldn't allow.

"It would make her feel permanent," Dr. Walsh said, "which is misleading. And it'd raise hell with Margaret."

That very day I typed "Nada Petrovich" on a piece of paper, cut it to size, and pasted it above one of the empty bottom pigeonholes. While I was still in the room, Margaret blasted around the counter, peeled the name-slip off, and tossed it into the trash.

"You have to clear that with Dr. Walsh," she said.

Margaret was a very petty woman.

Grace heard about the incident, as did Harper, and the two of them discussed it in my presence.

"Margaret *is* petty," Grace said, "deathly petty, but she doesn't have much either. It's when you have no place of your own, no power, that life is unbearable."

"Have you ever experienced that?" Harper asked.

"No," Grace said, "but any student of the world has to see it. Besides, my minor was psychology. It's a natural struggle between the old girls, and in this instance, Margaret has the right of way."

She had just freshened her lipstick, and her tiny bow mouth reminded me of a Fitzgerald woman, in a time when wit and intelligence made a path through a chaotic world. Wit is a weapon. It might win a bit of freedom but it can also block escape.

I asked, "Doesn't one have a duty to rescue?"

"That depends," Grace said. "The victim may prefer to be left alone."

"We're talking about a form of name tag. Just an acknowledgment of her presence—the most basic of rights."

She looked at me quite fondly. That was no pretense, I'm certain.

"You're right," she clipped. "Good for you, Arthur."

Harper raised his brows, pressed his fingertips together. He blew me a phantom kiss, an act I could neither interpret nor respond to, and then looked back at Grace.

"And here I thought you were Nada's ace in the hole," he said. "I'll have to reconstruct the situation."

"Don't try to understand me," Grace replied. "I can outthink both of you."

⌒

I asked Nada to lunch. Maybe it was the small gesture of a cowardly man, but it was public acknowledgment. I asked her in front of Margaret, I escorted her down the hall, and I took her to the Crossing. She was inordinately pleased. Coy. Coquettish. She talked about herself when pressed to do so: convent childhood, many jobs—one mapping residential lots for a government office—no family, but "a gentleman caller during holidays." She wanted to be a professor.

"Maybe I could teach creative writing," she said. "Like you. Then I could get a good job without a Ph.D. The English department might even hire me."

She was obviously oblivious to her age, to the possibility that, at seventy-something, she wouldn't have time to realize any of her goals; and oblivious, as well, to her own nonexistence. She thought she mattered. She didn't understand that they would never, never allow her to occupy more than cracks. I wondered why she couldn't see that? Why would she crawl around licking crumbs?

"Do you have a key to the office?"

"That Margaret's been talking to you."

"Do you?"

"Nobody can get a key without a key card. Dr. Walsh and Dr. Hirsch have to sign for it. They would never do that for me."

She had one. I can read gaps, too.

Before we left, I explained that I couldn't get a mailbox for her. "I'm too new," I said, "and I carry no weight. Not yet, anyway."

She invited me to her home for Thanksgiving. "No one should be alone on the holidays," she said.

She was a busybody, but still seemed the most totally unthreatening creature I'd ever known. I thought if she were an animal, she'd be a nibbler, maybe a wild-eyed meerkat, scanning the world for danger, herding the young back to the burrow, working and working.

⟶

Some species, you know, only *seem* to be good with their young. Take lionesses, the golden heroines. Let the male be killed and the female will sit idly by while the next contender chomps her babies to bits.

⟶

Imagine this: An old lady creeps across a lawn on a dreary Thanksgiving day, up onto the porch of a grand white house, with guests mingling inside. She lays before the door a cornucopia filled with apples, oranges, nuts, and cranberries. She creeps away again and spends Thanksgiving all alone.

That's what happened.

"Nada has struck again, I see." Grace held her cigarette to my lighter. "My God, that woman will be the death of us all."

"Maybe it wasn't Nada," Paul Harper said.

"Of course it was. She's probably across the street behind someone's house watching us this very moment."

Paul ambled down the walk as if looking for Nada, and in a moment Grace trailed after him. Grace had an angular way of flirting, elbow in palm, hip braced outward, head back, and that quick, bell-like laugh. She couldn't not flirt. Perhaps she wasn't even conscious of it. I could believe that.

"What makes Grace think Nada left the cornucopia?" I asked Carl. "Anyone could have done it."

"She's probably right. Nada probably heard about the dinner and wanted to be invited."

"Is she ever invited? To any of the department functions?"

"Sure, to the general ones. Nada just doesn't understand about divisions between faculty and staff. Or, more accurately, faculty and students. I'd rather bend the rules. But most people don't like being pushed."

"She invited me for Thanksgiving."

"She does that. She invites people and I guess waits for their return invitation."

"Did she invite you?"

"Not this year, but she has. Arthur, you shouldn't worry too much about Nada. She's a pretty happy woman, I think."

"I know. Though I'm not sure how she manages it. Her salary must be a joke. Sixteen hours, and probably minimum wage."

Loeffle didn't answer. I recognized the silence of an uneasy man.

"It can't be *less* than minimum wage, can it?"

"You'd have to talk to the Chair about that. I try not to get involved in budget matters." He looked sheepish. "She can really be a pest, you know. I like her, but she's got some funny ways."

"Is she bright? No one ever mentions anything good about her."

"I didn't mean to put her down. And yes, she is bright. Very much so. But once she gets locked on something, she can ruin a class. She insists on having her say. She once kept Harper's class tied up for thirty minutes on one word."

"What was it?"

"The word?"

"Yes."

Carl cocked his head, puzzled. "I don't know. Maybe I never asked. I just heard about it secondhand and it sounded like something she'd do. It's chilly out here, isn't it?"

He went inside and in a moment, Paul and Grace followed him. Grace paused, held the screen door open, and looked at me expectantly. "Coming in?"

"In a moment," I said.

"You just have to look for her, don't you?" She waited a moment more, as if she might have changed my mind, and then she closed the door.

I remained on the porch a while, my eyes scouring the neighborhood. It all seemed *so* wrong—all those happy people inside, Carl Loeffle contented with a brick-ugly wife, Grace fairy-dusting the small, exclusive gathering. Little carved niche for perfect people. All happy. And Nada, outside, bearing unwanted gifts. That was sad.

⟵

I know Nada left the cornucopia, because she wouldn't say she didn't. She talked circles around my questions in that meandering way women have, letting you understand the truth without their having to say it.

"What makes you think I did that?" she said.

"Dr. Burch said it was you."

"And what else did she say?"

"Nothing much. Just that it was you."

"People should give gifts on holidays."

"You could have rung the doorbell."

"You know better than that."

"It was a nice gesture. Let me thank you for everyone."

She paused at the doorway, one hand against the frame, and then bent her head quickly and left. A few moments later a lavender blur came through the door, whispered in my ear, "You be careful of that Grace. She's insatiable, you know, and she likes to have one waiting," and was immediately gone. A few days later, she approached me again, smiled conspiratorially, and said, "Dr. Harper borrows other people's ideas and writes papers about them. So you be careful." She patted my forearm and I placed my hand over hers.

"What do you whisper about me? To the other professors?"

"Nothing." She withdrew her hand. "I'm reading your book again, in case I missed something."

"You don't like it much, do you?"

"Yes I do. I do. But it's all people talking, you know? All dialog. I write, too. But not like you." She worried one wrist as if twisting a bracelet. "Your book is very good, very good. I like the young men very much. They're terribly sad. I just miss the *writer* talking to me, describing all the corners and shadows and how people feel."

"Sentiment."

She nodded. "That's the word. I like sentiment." She waited, probably for me to ask her about her own writing. Then she whisked on down the hall.

⟜

Nada wasn't alone in wanting sentiment. Most people do. I like it too. But it doesn't have to gush up out of the gutters to be recognized. It can be subtle—hard-earned and therefore better. At least, I hope it's better that way. I think women want it heavy-laden so they can absorb it without effort. They fortify themselves with sentiment. How else could they believe that they are innately lovable, permanently dear, and that the ravages of time will not alter one's devotion to them?

⟜

My manuscripts continued to dribble back. Rejected and rejected.

⟜

I asked Jack Goff, the young artist, to return my copy of *Fathers*. He apologized for not yet having read it. "It's been a bad semester," he said.

He returned the book two days later, without comment.

He was shaming me, no matter how I looked at it. If he hadn't read it, he held me in contempt. If he had, he didn't like it—the best work I had ever done or would probably ever do.

⟜

See? I didn't do anything except try to be a decent human being. I detested Margaret, yes, but I didn't plan any kind of retribution. I *couldn't* plan like that. Even if I wanted to, I couldn't ever get the channels open. Things had to happen on their own. I was just an aging, bald man, willing to get along with everyone, floundering around trying to be better than I am, and getting no help at all. It was too much at one time in one place with no one taking any responsibility for anyone else.

CHAPTER 12

I wanted a car desperately when I was sixteen. My mother got frightened just talking about it. She wasn't afraid to *ride* with someone, so I didn't understand her fear. It was too general and arbitrary. Now, I believe she suffered from agoraphobia, and cars meant traveling too far—her own boundary was fairly limited. But maybe she was just afraid I'd leave. Once she said, "You want a car so you can squire girls around, I guess."

I insisted that wasn't the reason. "I could get our groceries. We could go places. Anywhere. Maybe some of the games."

"No. It's girls you want a car for."

"That's not true."

"Yes, it is. We can't afford it anyway."

"I could get a job."

"Doing what?"

"I don't know."

"You get any money, you save it for college. You're going to need it."

Later that day she tied her hair back with a white ribbon and put on lipstick. She hadn't done that in a long time. With the slightest care, she was beautiful, strikingly beautiful.

"You're a real handsome boy, Arthur," she said. "I imagine the girls like you."

She seemed vulnerable right then, though I wouldn't have thought of that word. "Was my father good-looking?" I asked.

"Yes," she said. "I guess you'd call him handsome."

"Who was he?"

She sat very still, and I thought she would actually tell me.

"Oh, I don't know," she said. "Why can't you leave that alone?" She left the room and got lost in one of her books.

She was intuitively astute. Then, I *would* have liked a girl. I think I believed that one normal turn could straighten out all the roads. If I had a car, I might date. If I dated, I'd have a girlfriend, and that would make my mother just a mother.

Kids pin their faith to such simple things.

She read about dungeons, madmen, madwomen, lovely ladies panting and screaming and always surviving. I guess I was the only hero she could muster up.

⟵

After high school, I got a job at the IGA grocery in town. For the first two weeks, I walked. Mrs. Sutton offered to drive me, even to lend me her car on some days, but I didn't want that temporary, sometime help. I wanted, of course, to be my own man. I bought a bike. Even that little bit of independence was wonderful. It was mine. I had worked and paid for it.

And I paid my mother a token small amount toward room and board. She hadn't asked for it. She even said, "You don't have to do that, Arthur."

"You said we're low, almost out of money."

"The lease ran out and nobody picked it up."

"You could sell some land. We don't use it and we don't need it."

"I don't want to sell. We don't have to do that. Not yet."

"I could go to college easy if you'd do it."

"I wouldn't have anything then, for hard times."

"I'd take care of you."

She made an ugly, snorting sound. I'd never heard that before. "You just take care of yourself," she said.

She took the rent, though, a paltry twenty dollars. I felt good about that, as if the house were truly mine, too.

⟶

I liked my employer, David Watson. He was a tall man, quietly and lazily good, not given to questions. He let me work as much as I wanted, even on weekends. I learned how to take inventory, stock and mark goods. Once I overheard a regular customer ask him to lend her fifty dollars for an attorney. He said, "I'll be glad to do it, Rachel. You should have done this a long time ago." He went right to the register. I watched him from the aisle. He took out more than fifty. I wasn't there the day she paid him back, but I know she did. When she bought groceries, she always had a warm, "Hello, Mr. Watson," for him. I know good people when I see them, but maybe that doesn't mean a hell of a lot.

When I finally brought home a car, my mother came onto the porch. It was February and deep cold. The fields were an expanse of white under gray skies. She wore a brown cotton dress, rubbed her thin arms.

"So you did it. Good. You got some gumption."

She wanted to go for a drive immediately. She donned a short black coat and trudged in low flat shoes to the car.

She didn't want to go far, just to the highway juncture, to the gas station where, on summer Friday nights, local men held fish fries, and on winter nights they simply congregated, smoking and talking.

"You can buy me a soda, just like we were on a date."

I did buy her one, an orange. She sipped it on the way back home. The headlights sheared winter-bare trees. It was pleasant. She seemed very happy, but she said, "Guess you'll be leaving now. I'll be sorry to see you go."

That turned everything around, made the car and all possibilities sour and sad.

I was afraid to leave and I don't know why. We have to gather up our courage and take tiny leaps, tests of ability. It took me a long time. Sometimes, on my days off, I would drive to the state university at Wilshire. It, too, was a small town, about the size of Mason, only far more charming. I would pretend that I was a student, and already familiar with the place. I had lunch in their Union, browsed the bookstore, sat by the fountain. I drove through residential areas by the river and chose the site of my apartment. I even entered an apartment house once, climbed the stairs to the third floor. The carpet was pale brown with a faded pink-and-yellow rose pattern. I wanted the turret room, 4C. I returned to my car and imagined my future self strolling up the sidewalk, checking the mailbox for apartment 4C. Then I drove home, all afire to strike out on my own, be that guy entering the building where he lived alone.

But the good feeling just dissipated, like smoke. I found myself nearing home with a paralyzing heaviness and a deep tremble. It wasn't the kind of tremble that anyone sees. It's deeper than the muscles, maybe in the blood. I thought maybe the Arthur Blume who would live in that building was a crippled little rat, slimy and undone from the first. He'd get there, and he'd fail, miserably, not even have a maybe left.

So I began to delay the return home, to remain in the periphery of Wilshire. I found a small park just outside the city. It was set down from the highway, not easily accessed, and in rainy season might have been too marshy for most visitors' comfort. It was charming, serene, dotted with small ponds connected by narrow, shallow channels, and here and there little arched bridges crossing the channels. I didn't like bridges, but these were as much decorative as functional, some only three or four feet across, all with railings.

I stopped there during twilight hours when the heavy air suffused with change. I strolled the grounds, sat on a small, concrete picnic table, my feet on the bench. The solitude was soothing.

One afternoon, I saw a woman come down one of the entrance paths. Her car was parked on the rim above, and no one seemed to be in it.

She wore dark shorts, white kneesocks, and a white sleeveless blouse cut deeply inward to reveal broad shoulders. She had a lovely frame. Her blonde hair was pulled tightly back from a square, quite pretty face. No makeup.

As I headed for my car, our paths crossed. She smiled at me and nodded. "Hello," she said. It's a custom in the South to acknowledge another person, but usually women avert their eyes. I wished I had spoken to her. I turned and walked backward a few steps, wondering if she would glance after me. She didn't. I moved into the shade and waited beneath a linden tree. Its branches drooped and the deep green leaves were so broad, one alone could have hidden my face.

She was so pleasant to watch—very graceful, nimble. She strolled slowly, paused on bridges, maneuvered down the rock banks to toss twigs or small pebbles into the water. Night settled and she still lingered. Anyone could have been in the park with her.

When she finally left, she came my way. She walked leisurely, head bowed, fingers playing with a twig. She was deep in thought and probably very happy, very content with herself. I couldn't think of anything to say. I was very young. Words are never enough, anyway. When she saw me, her face registered first calm recognition, then a spasm of concern.

I walked by her though I wanted to stay. I wanted *her* to stay. She had a smattering of freckles on her fine shoulders. I went home.

⌐

I finally began classes at Wilshire, and it was joy enough to walk the grounds, to be so nearly one of a community. When the opportunity presented itself, I talked with fellow students after class, only briefly, about subjects we studied. Like the others, maybe more than they, I loved the intrigue of intellectual pursuit. They questioned a professor's statement that a person did not *have* knowledge if he could not express it so another person might understand it. It's a good question, and likely unanswerable.

My first writing class was in a long room with two doorways, each opening onto the same hallway. About twenty of us sat around six tables forming a square, so we could look at one another when critiquing manuscripts. Seated near one doorway was a young woman with freckles, blue eyes, and thick black hair, long and wildly curly. She was animated, argumentative, but usually correct. One couldn't help but watch her. In the middle of one class period, a stocky fellow at my end of the table arose, went out one door and came in the other, right behind the Medusa. He plunged his hands into the mass, tousling it fiercely, as he said, "I've wanted to do that all semester." Everyone laughed, including the victim and the professor.

My hands burned to be thrust in that moment, where his were, assuaging so sharply a desire. I imagine I laughed with the others.

Sometimes I see images of women in distress. The images can come to me at anytime. There's no dialog, no sound at all. Sometimes a black-and-white shot, sometimes color. The women don't look alike, which I assume is deliberate.

Some women are beautiful and some are ugly. I'm sympathetic with both, and anyone who studied my history would have to concede that.

Once upon a time a slight man tried to escape himself in a small park. He sat alone. He kept his back to the roadside paths so anyone approaching would know he preferred to keep his face and the entire rest of him to himself. But someone came and sat at his table and twitted a few inane sentences toward him. He turned around and joined her. Enjoined her. Her name *may* have been Gabby. She may have been some father's darling. And is no more.

That *could* have been the case.

At first I went home every weekend. But I began going less often, pleading the need for study time or rest time. My mother never argued with me. She never asked me to come home or not to leave. We managed her madness. I could make her eat, quiet down, and sometimes even rest. I often had to become Jesus, of course, and offer forgiveness for the tiniest compliance. She was pathetic. Beautiful and crazed. Not all the time, though. Just in and out, back and forth, as if she stumbled into it at 2:30 p.m. that particular day, or 12:00 midnight, or sunup. It always passed.

Late one Sunday evening, I drove back to Wilshire. I was morose, deeply so. As soon as I reached my apartment, I tumbled across the bed and fell asleep, weighted, unable to rouse and get into bed properly. When I woke, it was shortly after 3:00 a.m. My mouth was exceedingly dry, but my mind was peaceful. I could see Mrs. Sutton's face as clearly as if she had appeared in my room. She liked to walk early in the morning and usually followed the same route, just inside the back field by the road. Her dog had accompanied her till it died.

I had a bowl of cereal. Before me was the textbook for my afternoon class—we were reading *Don Quixote*. He was, of all fictional characters, the most lovable and most damned. He died, you know, not only stripped of the practice of his dream, but of belief in it. I washed the cereal bowl, showered, and dressed.

Then I went to my car and drove toward my hometown. When I turned onto the road leading back toward my mother's land, I slowed my pace. It was just dawn then. The sun washed the fields. Everything looks lovelier in the morning, like a new birth. The ground steams a little, as if it's shaping. I could have been going home in some future time, happier.

I stopped the car at Sutton's acreage and got out. Someone could have come by—that road can have heavy traffic. If they had, I would have gone back to Wilshire. But no one did. I can't help that. I saw her at the top of the long slope upward, walking in alignment with the fence. I was fond of her. She'd been good to me and even kinder to my mother. I crossed to the fence, taking some care to place my feet on rocky patches. When she saw me, she waved and walked toward the fence. She had one hand on her hip.

"I thought that was you, Arthur," she said, directly across from me, not more than two feet. "You headed back to Wilshire?"

"I wondered if I could use your phone."

"Yours out? Sure, come on." She gripped the overwire between the barbs and pressed down, leaning her body weight forward to lower the fence for me. So she had always done, allowing me brief respite.

On my return to Wilshire, I stopped at one of the small inner parks and waded into a pond. The water was cold and cleansing. I sat on a wooden bench with wrought iron legs and let the sun dry me. A few geese were on the pond and I admired their double swimming. They have ornate, beautiful rituals. Each knows precisely how to behave.

If I had been in Cervantes's work, I would probably have been Sancho Panza. He was a very practical man.

Two policemen came to Wilshire to talk with me about Mrs. Sutton. They had talked with all the farmers in that area, and my mother told them I had been home for the weekend. One was terribly overweight, pasty and folding over himself, and sat on the sofa, while the other sat at the kitchen table with me, taking notes.

"Did you see anyone? A car or anything?"

"No. Nothing. I was tired, though, and was driving sort of automatically. I think I would've noticed anything unusual."

"What time did you get back here?"

"Maybe eleven or twelve. I'm not sure."

"Could anyone verify that?"

"You think I would hurt her?"

"I'm not accusing you of anything. You were in the area and we have to ask."

"It's fascinating. I can't imagine that anyone would think I could do something like that. I don't know. Maybe someone saw me come in. I guess I could ask."

"We'll do that."

"Could I come along?"

He closed his notebook. It was a small, breast-pocket pad. "No," he said. "I'll get back to you."

He did so, but not until about 6:30 that evening. He called me from the station. One tenant had seen my car in my parking space when he went out for beer. That was about midnight. Another had heard my shower at about 8:00 a.m. "It's not likely," the policeman said, "that you'd drive home, then turn around and drive back and back again."

"I knew Mrs. Sutton pretty well," I said. "She's a friend of my mother's. I know only good things about her. I can't imagine that anyone would want to hurt her."

"There's a lot of crazy people around."

A hunter had found Mrs. Sutton in a sitting position, leaning against a fence post. Her shirt was as red as poppies.

My mother could have been the one to find her, their properties were so close.

CHAPTER 13

MASON, FALL 1991

Many predators toy with game, especially if the predator is full, content, and has time. It's a different appetite that needs sating from time to time. Lions, monkeys. Anything that has evolved enough to clutch something else does it.

There's this female frog—a golden frog, ironically—that is *huge* in contrast with the male. The tiny mate, once he's mounted, can't get off. His belly melds to her back. Gradually, bit by bit, her body absorbs all he is, leaving the withered skin riding her like a dead baby slung onto her back.

And there's a minute male spider that twists his body into the poisonous fangs of his female partner so he dies in the moment of mating. The survivor turned predator, though, is the sea slug. The soft, vulnerable creature slips into the poisonous arms of the anemone, absorbs the poisonous stings, and slips away looking as innocuous as ever but armed with another's poison.

The natural world is no place for any creature, but there's no place else to go.

Grace ordered a copy of *Fathers* through an out-of-print bookstore and presented it to me at her home one Saturday. She was directly before me, hands behind her back like a child hopeful that a gift was pleasing. "Will you sign it for me?" she asked. "That tear was already there."

"I don't doubt it. It's been around a long time."

It was a good copy, no name in the cover, little wear, no discoloration, a state that to a writer is both blessing and curse. It was still handsome. But perhaps it had never been read, just purchased and put aside. It was a meager gift on both our parts, her purchase and my standing there having done so little else.

"It's a wonderful book, Arthur."

"You've read it?"

"Of course. Why would I buy it except to read it?"

I gave her real motives. "To support a colleague or to satisfy curiosity. Or just as a kindness?"

She shrugged. "Those aren't bad reasons. But they're not mine." The edge of her anticipation visibly vanished. "*Will* you sign it?" she urged.

She didn't understand. My hesitation wasn't idiosyncratic; it was practical. "Do you want only my name," I asked, "or an inscription of some kind?"

"Write what you feel like writing."

"Some people don't want a message, because they plan to give the book as a gift."

"I plan to keep it, Arthur."

"Then let me wait. I don't want to write it in a hurry."

"Okay."

I placed it on the glass coffee table. "It's not easy to know how to sign a book," I explained. "I used to think each person wanted me to write a personal note, but usually it's not the note they want, unless the writer is really famous. And if I use the word 'to' it makes me distant from the receiver. It's like a gift card on my own book. I should just begin with the name."

"It's all right, Arthur," she said. "I really don't mind."

If she didn't, then no wonder I didn't know what to write.

She told me she had truly enjoyed the book and wished she had read it before I arrived on campus. "I assumed it would be good," she said, "but it was also touching. It allows a special insight."

Outside her house, the day was blustery, a little cool, and the wind made slapping noises against one window, perhaps with a juniper branch. Everything in her home was too uniform, bland. She kept the drapes drawn, kept the house too warm. I didn't need her insight into my writing. Why would she confuse what I wrote with what I was? She was an educated woman.

"Fine," she said. "We'll talk about it some other time. We're not analyzing literature, after all, are we?"

She liked pleasantries and could smooth awkwardness with a turn of phrase. She also knew she had taken over my property, or had attempted to.

⟵

Women are selling themselves when they shop with a male companion. Grace was quick, and colorful, posing with earrings held to her shell ears, looking dismayed at slacks so long they buckled at her arches.

"Are you enjoying yourself, Arthur?" she asked.

Yes, I was. I sat in a chair just outside the dressing room and Grace entertained me with different versions of herself. Some of the passing women nodded to me. I was the saleswoman's darling.

Grace was beautiful. Dainty women can move like trinkets of light, trickles of sound, come catch me if you can.

I offered to buy her an outfit, but she brushed the gesture aside.

"Of course not," she said. "I'm the one who suggested shopping, and it wasn't so you would buy me something."

"But I would like to. Doesn't that matter?"

"Well," she looked appraisingly at me a second, "yes, it does, and thank you. Some other day, maybe. How's that? We'll go shopping expressly to let you buy a gift for me."

I conceded, though the concept of gift had changed. "All right."

"What's wrong with doing it that way?"

"Nothing."

"It's just too aboveboard, isn't it? Should I be coy?"

"Now you're belittling my gift."

"Maybe I am. Sorry."

She bought absolutely nothing then, and though her cheeriness resumed almost immediately, I understood that buying something now would attract too much attention from one or both of us. We would both be finely tuned on what she bought and why and that destroyed her own approach to shopping.

We had a late, slow dinner. Grace did not want to rush her leisure time. She favored the Algonquin Hotel because the thermostats really worked. She chilled easily. When she thought I was sleeping, she would flit like a slender ghost to the wall, then back to the bed. The air conditioner would stop or the heater would hiss. Maybe she knew I was awake, but if we didn't acknowledge what occurred, she could be guiltless. Her comfort mattered most.

The night of our first shopping excursion, I got out of bed after she was truly asleep. I opened the drapes so a shaft of moonlight fell across her and I watched the rise and fall of her breasts. She was, as I have said, beautiful and tiny. At night, asleep, she was a different being.

Of course I wondered what she thought of *Fathers*, the details, not her insight into me, but I also didn't want to know, at least not then. Some matters one gets *ready* to know.

We made love well, except that Grace would sometimes laugh and the night shattered. I like extreme, tense quiet.

↤

Women copy each other. They borrow clothing, have pots of makeup, creams, dilutions, dyes, wigs, false body parts. They modulate their voice, mimic walks, pretend pleasure. They may pretend everything, every minute, so every cell is a lie, every atom a trap. It takes a keen eye and a strong will not to waver.

↤

Some people dislike the fall of night. It's like the whole world goes to sleep and only the awake are vulnerable. A fellow might go to a convenience mart then and watch the little lives inside, watch entries, purchases, exits. Rain might veil the scene.

↤

Grace considered it her right to worry at me. She wanted to wander through my past and reconstruct her image of the man she chose to be with. I resisted her as much as I could.

"Arthur," she said one evening, "you're never specific. Never. You don't mention towns you've lived in, or people you've known. Nothing."

Her tone was playfully chastising, as if I too often forgot to turn out a light. "I don't deliberately *not* mention them," I said.

We were in her basement, trying to light the pilot of her furnace. I'm not adept with mechanical things, but I could read the directions clearly and her small hand maneuvered the lever and match appropriately. "Done!" She blew out the match, and stood, her mind still on point. "That may be true, but it's an odd trait. I've never known anyone who didn't give some details about himself."

"I don't assume people are interested in me. I've read that a good conversationalist asks questions, and I try to follow that guide. Besides, I thought my vita was open to everyone on the faculty and that you all examined it."

She was on the stairs ahead of me. I put my hands on her hips, and she said, "Hey, there," turning to look at me. "You're trying to change the subject."

"You're a nice subject."

"No digression," she warned. She went on up, quickly, continuing to pursue me. "I could have read your file, but who wants to read that dry stuff? Even when I'm on the Personnel Committee," she said, "I pay more attention to the interview, even a phone interview, than the written record. A voice can tell you a great deal."

"You've heard my voice."

"Yes, and I like it, as you well know." She tiptoed to bite my earlobe. "I like all of you, actually. But please stop changing the subject. Now, admittedly, I have resorted to reading your personnel file, but given that and all our conversations, this is what I know about you." She reiterated details from my vita, from my professional life. "And, the most personal so far," she said at the end, "other than what I've garnered through reading *Fathers*, which I believe is fiction, is that you were born and reared in Georgia."

"That's right."

"Where is the town?"

"Mid-Georgia."

She ticked off her next questions with finger against finger. "Did you live *in* town, within the city limits? Did you have any family in town? Of course, I know you had no brothers or sisters, because I've asked, but did you have cousins? Uncles? Friends? What about friends, Arthur? Give me a name of someone who was a buddy. I know about that Charles Bovary fellow and Juliette Preston. That was college. How about a girlfriend?" She bit her lower lip and raised her arched eyebrows. "Girlfriend?"

"That kind of question is beneath you. You don't really want to know."

"But I do. I really do. This is a serious conversation, Arthur."

"You keep your own affairs private, except for the occasional list."

She took me by the hand, led me to the sofa. The television screen flickered silently, some stylized, intense movie with a raft, floating down a jungle river. A man in armor, leaning on a sword, was looking at the sky. All around him swarmed monkeys. She would leave crazy things on the screen and pay them no mind whatsoever.

She continued to hold my hand. "What was your mother's name?"

"Why does that matter?"

"Just tell me. No questions, Arthur. Just answer me. What was your mother's name?"

I answered her question. "Mary."

"Truly? You're not just being symbolic and evasive?"

"My mother's name was Mary."

"*Was* Mary? So she's deceased?"

"Yes."

"When did she die?"

"A long time ago."

"What did she die of?"

Her voice had softened. She could do that, slip into an intimate, caring tone. She may have done that with students. She may have done that with every lover, with every person in her life, whenever she found it expedient.

"Arthur. What did your mother die of?"

"I would like not to continue with this, if you please. It makes me uncomfortable."

I never asked *her* for intimate details of her life, but she examined mine, even from the beginning. She read *Fathers* rooting for something. Rooting. That destroys the story. Some surfaces should be left intact. Common humanity demands it. I tried to warn her, to let her know I, too, had boundaries.

She nodded and relented. "So I see. And honestly, it makes me uncomfortable, too. I feel like the Grand Inquisitor. I just meant to let you know how very private you are, and how hard it is to be close to you. You shut me out."

"No, I don't. I meet most of your requests, and I'm happy to do that. I want to continue doing it. When you wish to go out, we do, when you wish to stay home, we do. I park up the street, because you don't want our relationship known. As far as all our colleagues know, I have no close friends here. That might work against me professionally, but I don't quibble. If you're uncomfortable acknowledging me, I'll be your secret."

"You have an odd take on things, Arthur."

"According to you," I said. "You have your own peculiarities, and I don't try to fathom them. I *accept* them."

She held my hand a little longer, ran her thumb absentmindedly over my knuckles, like little hills of thought.

"You may be right," she said. "You don't pry. You're an unusual guy."

"Thank you. I think."

"Yes, it's a compliment. Right now, anyway." She leaned forward and pressed her lips to mine. It wasn't a sensual kiss. It was loving. She put her hand against my cheek.

She had said, "Right now, anyway." What did that mean?

⤝

At the library, I located three of her articles and read them on the spot. She had an intelligent, clear prose style, with many transitions of thought, much evidence and interpretation, and occasionally that personal mark of humor couched in question form—"Could it be?" "Shall we believe?" I told her I admired her style and depth of research.

⤝

I wonder what my mother might have been like if she were sane. I wonder, too, if insanity overtook her or was born with her. A famous person, whose name escapes me now, once said that if a sane and an insane person live together, the insane will not become sane; the sane will become crazed.

But what if the condition is not constant? What if both natures are in one person? Does one overtake the other? If so, then there's a chance that the better will win out if one endures long enough.

I've looked for a gap in my reasoning, the transparency that supposedly can be spotted by any astute mind. It seems logical that even though I might not be able to fill the gap, I could *recognize* it. But if one exists, from every angle it eludes me.

⟿

I may meticulously note patterns and even recall them, but I don't make them. Things pop up. Twice I traveled by public transportation some distance—1,200 miles in one case, by train—and waited. The long trip was in August. I telephoned a college in Arkansas to see if Carla Jeffers still taught there and to verify her address. She had been pretty vicious to a writer I knew and respected. He didn't know me well—I was an adjunct instructor for the summer—but he spoke to me when we passed. "Hello, Arthur," he always said, as though we were equals, if not friends. Funny how good men are often tall. He was using Carla Jeffers's office while she was on semester leave. She still came to the office at times, and he was, I heard, particularly careful not to rearrange her office much. He added only one touch, a poster advertising an old western movie. It was in color: A buxom blonde woman lies against a sloping boulder, pinioned there by the left hand of an Indian. His right hand has ripped the bodice of her prim dress, and her supposedly virginal bosom swells in fear. Jeffers protested that art. She didn't care about the fellow's rights or his pride. The office was, at least temporarily, *his*.

She tried to have the lock to her office rekeyed, but the department chair balked. He asked me to let the gentleman professor have my office space; I could then move into Jeffers's and everyone would be saved some unpleasantness. I approached the writer and told him I was hesitant to participate in the exchange, because he might believe I had taken Jeffers's side, which wasn't the case. He told me not to worry, that no one need move at all. The next morning he had put a hand-printed sign on the door. It announced that his office hours, for the rest of the semester, and perhaps the rest of the year, would be held in the northwestern corner booth of the Mexican restaurant in the union cafeteria. He was, and is, an excellent writer and an excellent man.

When I arrived at the Arkansas town where Jeffers lived, I took a taxi to an address three blocks away, then walked to her house. She had loved to tell tales about her dog. It slept inside, in her bedroom. It was late at night, not my favorite time. I slipped on gloves. I crawled through the dog-door from the backyard into the garage. I got in her car. I even dozed a little. In the morning, when the door to the house opened, I lay quietly, hearing the dog-door flap and the house door close. Then I emerged very cautiously, and lowered the wooden panel that would keep the dog shut out.

I went in the house and surprised her in the kitchen. She got hit in the head with a skillet, which had been on the stove. She was hit many times. She was a mess. Her underwear was removed, though I had no interest in her that way. But let people wonder and conjecture on a nature that isn't mine. She had pill bottles lined along the kitchen window and they were dumped on her body. Some of them floated in blood. Unravel that. In the bathroom mirror, I checked my face for blood. I walked out the front door, up the street to a bus stop, and then rode city buses until it was time for my train to leave.

I know I was seen one or two times and that a description of some strange man may have appeared in a newspaper or in a newscast. But no one since Wilshire ever came to call and question. I never soiled my own nest. I had no connections with these women, and the span of time between my even knowing them and my final encounter with them made me, if not invisible, inconsequential.

Once a name is out, it's out. I wouldn't deliberately keep secret something the world already knew.

CHAPTER 14

MASON, DECEMBER 1991

I wasn't blind to Nada's flaws, but I chose not to magnify them. People have this tendency to excuse their own foibles but to find no excuse for the other fellow's weakness. I admit she was a pest, a little filled with herself. She wanted me to read an entire notebook of her poems even though she wasn't a student of mine, and even though I had reams of papers to go through every week, to respond to conscientiously. I told Nada her work would have to wait. The notebook did pique my interest, since she said it was "one of many." Her hand swept a vast wall of notebooks.

"I've written volumes," she said. "My whole life."

"Since what age?"

She shrugged in a manner that females sometimes use, a mild ploy. She was wearing a blue print dress with a false collar to fill the extreme dip of the bodice. With the shrug, her ample bosom rose, powdery and oversoft.

"Twelve," she said. "Or even younger."

She had to have been a beauty in her youth and I was perplexed how she had come to be here, still striving.

"Will you read them?" she insisted.

"Every word of your entire life?"

"That's not what I mean," she said, and huffed away. She respected me, but she didn't fear me. I wanted to help her and she knew that.

Grace said they were probably "diary jottings." "God," she said, "can you imagine her whole life in her own words? Might be an entertaining read."

"They were more than jottings. They were poems. I saw the first few."

"Poems? That's even worse. Let's see." She stood straight and primly, with her hands clasped in front of her. "A poem by Nada Petrovich. 'The white lily reaches its pale arms to the waning moon.'"

I laughed, though I didn't really find it amusing. And I liked the line Grace had just authored. It's the kind of thing I've always had trouble writing. I can think it, but I'm afraid it'll sound syrupy. Feminine.

"Don't ever let me hear that you're reading Nada's poems," I responded. "Your sole purpose would be to ridicule."

She was wrong to debase Nada and her work and wrong to charge me with her own flaws. I never sneered at Nada in any way.

⌒

At Christmas, Nada brought large bowls rounded with fruit; candy dishes filled with hard candy, tiny balls, and squares, striped and solid.

"I don't eat candy, Nada," I said.

"I know. But it looks so pretty. And you *might* have some. People change."

"I don't."

"Now don't say that. You don't want to limit yourself, do you? People shouldn't do that. Besides, I like doing this."

Hum. Bustle. Swish that dust, shine that bowl. Hum. Curls bouncing. Oh happy holidays down the hall.

On my office door she fashioned a Christmas tree of old greeting cards. She carefully cut out only the pictures, leaving no printed or written messages. I thus had a tree of holiday scenes hovering over pictures of gifts. She was clever. She could make do with nothing. And as far as I could determine, she hadn't done so for anyone but me. I didn't see a sign of Nada in Loeffle's office, or Harper's, or Grace's, or Walsh's. She had concentrated her efforts on me. It was touching. Gaudy, maybe, but a genuine effort to please.

I bought her a royal-blue silk scarf and she opened the package in front of me, wore the scarf around her neck the rest of that day and for the rest of the week. "Dr. Blume gave this to me," I heard her say numerous times.

Carl Loeffle said, "That was a nice thing to do, Arthur. The department should give her something, I guess."

"Yes. She certainly does enough for people here."

Loeffle didn't follow through, though. Or someone put the quietus to the idea.

Margaret, aping monkey, apparently liked Nada's primitive tree. She copied the idea. It was a flop. From red construction paper, she made bell-shaped name cards for each member of the department—forty, counting graduate assistants, instructors, student aides, and so on—and used them to outline a tree on a blank wall. It was suitable, maybe, for elementary minds.

"You can tell," Paul Harper said, "your favor in the office, at least with our Margaret, by your position on the tree."

My name was on the branch third from the top.

"Not bad for a new man," Harper said, following my gaze.

His own was on the top branch. "Chocolates." He smiled.

I looked for the others, Loeffle, Grace, Walsh. Then I saw Nada's—at the very bottom of the lowest branch.

"I wonder if Nada has seen this."

"You can bet on it. She doesn't miss a trick."

I waited till Margaret was on her lunch break. Then I exchanged Nada's name tag with mine.

Nada came to my office later. "I know you moved my name to the top of the tree. Thank you."

"You're welcome. I'll see that it stays there."

"I know you probably have some place to be for Christmas," she said, "but if you don't, I'd be happy for you to come to my house."

"I appreciate your offer. But I do have plans."

"I thought so. A man like you. I have a guest coming anyhow, a gentleman friend of mine. So I won't be alone. I'm never alone during the holidays. But if you change your mind. . . ."

"I probably won't. If I do, I'll certainly come. You've got a generous spirit. Thanks."

She swirled away.

Later that day, Nada's bell was gone. Completely. Margaret was at her keyboard, but she was aware of me. The air charges sometimes, and I know everyone feels the current. I walked behind the counter to stand right beside Margaret. I recall the fat grossness of her forearms, the pinkness of her ears. I saw a woman once whose ears had been sliced off. I didn't do it. It was in a book on old-time punishments.

She glanced up but continued to type. "Yes?"

"Why do you do petty things like that? Move the tag?"

"Nada shouldn't even be on the tree. I just made her a bell to be nice."

"Why shouldn't she have one? Everyone else does. All the assistants."

"Nada's no assistant." Her voice was lilting. Saying those words delighted her. She typed away.

"Certainly she is. Maybe she's not a teaching assistant, but she's a research assistant. She a part of this department and office and entitled to share in any celebration we have. I don't understand why you pretend she doesn't belong."

She punched something on the keyboard and the screen gurgled like water had filled it. She stood up and met my eyes. Hers were beady and bloodshot and, oddly, triumphant. "She's *not* an assistant," she pronounced. "She's just a student. She *volunteers* her time and *pretends* she gets paid for it."

She walked away, steamed up and righteous. She had a nasty twitch to her walk. She was so happy to have been forced into telling me what I wasn't supposed to know.

Without thinking, I followed her. I didn't want to let her go. Never had I wanted so much not to let someone go. She was in the copy room. I didn't approach her. I just watched her. When she went back to her desk, I followed, and again just stood a few feet from her. My class hour came, but I didn't move. She looked at the clock and at me. Professors and instructors checked their mail, talked.

Someone said, "Are you all right, Arthur?"

"Yes. Very. Margaret isn't."

"I'm fine," she said. When they left, she went into the Chair's empty office and closed the door. I could imagine her in there, chewing her nails, frightened but elated. I had to go to my class and I did so. I always do what I have to do. I apologized to them for being late.

At 5:00 p.m., I stood on the west side of the building, at the bottom of the steps. Margaret came out, buttoning her coat. She saw me.

"What are you doing?" she said.

I didn't answer.

Cold winter wind, gusts of mist-like sleet. Fat Margaret, sturdy and worried, arms folded. Arthur Blume, wanting direction. Let it be Margaret.

When her ride came, I went back to my office and waited until silence indicated I was alone. Then I sat at Margaret's desk and made another tag for Nada. So ridiculous. A grown man, sitting in an empty office fashioning a bell out of construction paper. I replaced Margaret's tag with Nada's. I put the scraps of red paper on Margaret's desk and placed the scissors on top. I wrote a note and laid it on the scissors. "May the spirit of Christmas reward you."

And still, I was sick. It wasn't enough. I wanted to *act* and I couldn't, because this was my present tense. I had to live here, work here, succeed here. But I couldn't count on justice; justice for people like Margaret never comes soon enough.

I was locking the door behind me when I heard "Dr. Blume," and turned to see Nada herself.

"I need to turn this paper in to Dr. Walsh," she said. "I was hoping someone would still be in there."

She hurried by me and when she emerged again, I knew she'd checked out the tree.

"Nobody's ever been as kind to me as you have," she said.

I kissed her forehead and walked away.

"You're a sweet man," I heard. She came to the top of the steps and called it after me again. "You're a real sweet man, Dr. Blume."

⟶

The Chair called me in. "What's this between you and Margaret?"

"Nothing, really. She's irritated because I chastised her, pretty mildly, I think, for refusing to let Nada's name be included in the office decorations. They do represent us all, don't they? The decorations?"

"Yes. She left Nada off?"

"*Removed* her name. Twice."

"She didn't tell me that."

"I didn't think so. It's no big thing. It's over now."

"Margaret says you followed her around the other day."

"You're kidding."

"No. She said she had to wait ten or more minutes for her husband, and the whole time you eyed her 'like a bulldog.' Her exact words."

"That sounds like Margaret. I was just preoccupied, I guess, with a personal problem. She was probably feeling guilty. And she should."

He nodded. "Yes. She goes too far." He wasn't through, though. I could see him searching for phrases. He was about my age, but pasty and intellectual, with weak, red lips, and with an obvious dislike of the distasteful. "You heard about what happened? That Margaret's cat is missing? Its collar was left on her car."

"I heard that. Someone really had it in for her."

"She believes you did it."

I told him I was sorry anyone could even think that way. He felt the same. He was as shocked and disgusted by the whole business as I was. He said he'd speak to Margaret later about the way she treated Nada. "She just wants to be in total control," he said. "You know how it is."

⌒

Grace explained about Nada's position, though she didn't tell me the whole truth.

"You're messing with a woman's pride now," she said. "Don't ask Nada questions."

"Is she paid or not?"

"Yes, but it doesn't go through the department budget so Margaret doesn't know."

"So, in order to make Margaret feel good bullying Nada, you all keep a lie on the surface."

"Jesus, you're obsessed with that woman."

"No I'm not. I'm obsessed with honesty and justice."

"Get off your high horse, Arthur. How can you stand Nada? I feel sorry for her, too, but there's a limit. She's in your office whenever she wants. It reflects her personality more than yours. It looks like Nada's parlor."

"It makes her happy and it doesn't bother me."

"It really doesn't, does it? Well, who knows what *does* bother you. You're not exactly a forthright person, you know."

"And you would want me to be?"

"Hmmm," she said. "Maybe not." She studied me quietly for a moment. That was one of her ways, an absentminded perusal, as if a person had taken her on a tangent, made her weigh a portentous matter.

What I said wasn't nearly as important as what I didn't say. She had black eyes. A beautiful, tiny, precise woman. Her voice was bigger than she was.

～

Justinia called me after midnight during the first week of December, when students were staying in trying to make up for a semester of lethargic thought and dilatory effort. It was the week of finals, test time, passage.

"I'm at the Club," she said. Her voice was muffled. She was sniffling. "I need a ride and I don't want anyone up front to see me. Could you come get me? Come round back."

I didn't mind. I dressed hurriedly and slung on a jacket. Outside was an icy rain, quite silvery. The Club, where Justinia danced for her own pleasure and for that of others, was about five miles outside town. Its neon light glowed enough territory for a carnival, which was appropriate. Only three cars were in the lot. When I drove around the back of the low building, Justinia sprang from the door as if she had been holding it ajar. She had on a jacket, leather I learned soon, that didn't cover her from mid-hip on down. She was nude underneath. She plopped into the car, shuddered "Thanks," and scrunched down into the seat. Under the false light, she was blue. Her cheek bone was swollen, cut.

"Do you want to go to the police?"

She shook her head vehemently.

"Shall I take you home?"

"No. I don't want to be alone."

Justinia may have been frightened or angry, but who could tell? She didn't succumb to power, even of feelings. Before we even reached my apartment building, she was sitting more erect, had drawn her hands from the pockets and was clutching the jacket around her.

"Got myself in a mess, old Bloomin' Arthur."

"So I see." I pulled off into a dark driveway. "Don't be alarmed," I said. I got out, removed my coat, and passed it to her. She took off the jacket she was wearing and tossed it out the window.

"Is that his?"

"Yep. I grabbed it and ran."

"You might want to take it to the police."

"No. He's just a pervert. I broke the rules. We're not supposed to leave with the customers."

"Why did you?"

"I don't know." Then, "He wasn't just a customer."

I took her up to my place. While she bathed, I stood at the living room window. The outside had a silver sheen. Somewhere her attacker was thinking of her or forgetting her. Either way, she was central, even in her absence. It was a paradox I had thought of often.

I let Justinia wear my robe.

"I like this robe," she said.

"You look good in it, but you may not have it."

"How did you know I wanted it?"

"It's a nice robe, and, as I said, it's becoming. Or, rather, you're becoming to it."

"But you want to keep it?"

"Yes."

I fixed her a cup of tea not because she liked tea—I was certain she didn't—but because my action was comforting to her.

"The pervert," she said, "is in Life Drawing. He's been after me."

"Which is what you wanted, I imagine."

"Sort of. Not *him*. I thought some of them would get, you know, aroused."

"That's not the purpose of the class."

"I know, but how can they help it?" She looked somberly at me. She really wanted an answer. "I know," she said, "that I have a good body."

"Yes you do, but a man can have other interests."

"Even when I'm *naked*?"

"Especially then. Did Jack get aroused?"

"If he did, he did a good job of hiding it."

"A man can do that, too," I said. "Maybe Jack is one of them."

That pleased her. She nodded. "I hope the pervert drops the class."

"You could see to it that he does."

She considered that. "Nope. And don't you do it, either."

"You don't want me to champion you?"

She shook her head. "Not over this."

We slept side by side in the same bed, with no other intimacy. In the night, I pulled the covers up over her exposed shoulders.

I think I respond genuinely well to genuine pain.

—

The hunter's cabin on my mother's land was a rough timber building with two windows like glass paraffin that turned the inside into gray smoke. In one corner a long, narrow box with a hinged lid served as storage and bed. The mattress was ticking filled with straw or cornhusks. It rustled when I lay down on it. I could sleep there in the daytime, unless the men were about.

In quail season, I sometimes squatted at the rim of the field and watched the men flush their prey into flight. Shots cracked the morning. Some of the men stuffed birds in their game pouch without checking whether they were yet dead. Others had ways of dispatching them quickly. One man, broad as the doorway to the shack, bit the throat of the quails, and wiped his mouth with the back of his hand.

"You're going to get shot," my mother said. "They're fools when they're hunting."

I wondered if she had ever watched what they did, but I didn't ask her. I didn't want to rile her, even to gain information.

CHAPTER 15

CHRISTMAS, 1991

Grace wanted me to leave with her during the Christmas break, to go to Jackson, Mississippi, where she'd be visiting friends. I explained that I didn't like being an outsider during the holidays.

"You'll be with *me*," she said, standing before her fireplace, though she had not started a fire. "But, still, I can understand not wanting to be around a group with a history you don't share. Let's go somewhere else. Anywhere. I'll pay for the tickets."

"I can pay my own way."

"I know you can, but I also know that thanks to my father, I have a wee bit more money than most people. Besides, I'm the one who wants you to go. Let me," she twirled around, "entertain you."

"I can't. I'm sorry."

"Come on, Arthur. Mason is a miserable place during the holidays. It's a closed community. Everyone either leaves or draws into their family—you know how that is."

"I need to send out my new book, circulate some queries. A block of free time is very precious to me."

"You could send out your manuscript in one day."

"No, I can't."

"Two at the most."

"You have no idea how long it takes. And I want to write, start something new. Maybe even read a little."

She plopped down in the corner of the loveseat, diagonal from the sofa where I sat. She could thus look directly at me. "What I suspect," she said, "is that you'd rather do anything but be with me for more than a few hours."

"I do want to be with you. But I have a life, too, separate from you. I've just made a realistic assessment of what I must do and when I have time to do it. It's the approach *you* usually take."

She didn't answer for a moment. "Is that true?"

"Yes."

"Okay," she said. "It does sound right." She leaned forward, elbows on knees, her hands cupping her face. "Since we're talking truth here, let me ask you for another bit of honesty."

I waited.

"If we're not hitting it off, would you just take the bull by the horns and tell me so? I'm tired of trying to read how you feel, and I don't want to embarrass myself."

"We hit it off very well. We're just not alike."

"So what does that mean?"

"I'm sure I'm a constant disappointment to you, like now. And I'll probably continue to be. I can't meet your needs, not all of them."

"You meet some very, very well."

"But that's not enough, is it? Isn't that what we're discussing? I don't want you to be unhappy. Truly. I don't want you unhappy."

She was pleased again.

"Okay. You've made your case. Maybe I've been a bully. It's been known to happen." She moved over by me, leaned across me so I could see her face and we could kiss.

"Could we go away just for two days? Now?"

I had just said "No," many times.

"Hear me out, please? We could take a train to Union Station in St. Louis, do a little shopping, spend the night in a nice hotel, and come back the very next day. Then I'll fly off and stay away until January third, and never, never, present you with any recriminations. It can be my Christmas present."

"We could drive there in half the time."

"I know, but you wouldn't do it, would you? Besides, then one of us would have to drive and would miss the scenery and the rest. Do come. Please. It will get you out of town, and a train ride is such a treat for people who like to read. We can sit in the smoker car, have a drink, play cards, or not. You could even edit a manuscript while we travel, or draw up an exam, or look up markets. I don't know. But the station—it's grand and old. Beautiful. I don't know how big it really is, but it's like a little town inside a building. Movies, boutiques, restaurants, export shops, crafts, street vendors—only I guess they're station vendors, huh? Or mall vendors?—Anyway. There's a fudge factory, and the candy makers—they're all college kids—stop and sing often, a four-part harmony thing. You know how much fun little things can be. Come on, Arthur. Please."

We drove separately to Kansas City, so she could go directly to the airport upon our return. She led the way and I kept her car in view, though I didn't shift lanes as she did. She may have slowed down for me to catch up. I knew where the station was, of course, but the secret, strained togetherness was part of the package. I parked a block away from the station and walked in from the opposite side. That much of my travel was my own. Grace was buying the tickets. I waited outside. This station was small, set down in a little pit-like dip. I wasn't in a holiday mood and neither was that part of the city. The buildings were humdrum, and trash skittered along the walkways.

I tried to enter Grace's mood. I was willing, but sometimes all good just suspends itself and a fellow has to wait till it flows on again. The landscape flew by, the sun flashed against bits of remaining ice. Light sliced through the windows, over the seats. I liked the smoker, because it was an upper tier, and we could see the coming terrain, be on top of the speeding machine, not passengers so much as riders. But Grace didn't like the smoker car after all, and we returned to the plusher recliners. She read, and occasionally had to read a line *to* me. "Listen to this." "Oh, Arthur, you must hear . . . "

I read, too, and when I wanted to share a passage, I passed her the book, pointing at the particular lines, but still, she had to read *aloud* to me. She liked hearing her own voice. For a short time she fell asleep and her head rested on my shoulder. I wondered what my life would be like if she were really mine, and we would be together again and again and again. Every day. She would bubble life as she did, and breathe warm against my skin. I took her hand and studied her unpolished nails, filed into delicate ovals. They were the hands of a simple person, perhaps a child. But when I leaned forward, to glimpse her face, I saw how the flesh around her eyes sagged down, her cheeks slackened into mild jowls. And there was the bright red bow mouth. I had seen her look even worse, though she probably didn't know that. When an older woman is above one, looking down, even with affection and more, the flesh of her face falls forward, and the eyes stay back.

Once an image is in the mind, it can surface anytime, and you know it's no dream because you saw it. It lives inside you.

I turned my gaze away, to the window. Here I was, speeding away from my home, from my safety, with someone who would own the whole day, the whole night, and tomorrow too, every minute, every second. I couldn't return until we had completed her jaunt. And if I did, if I *did*, she would change into something else, and where would we be? What could she do to me? I would have to move on, start over, try again. Her bow mouth, her sweet ways. It was enough to stop my breath.

She woke and sat up, looked at me. "I fell asleep, it's so nice. Did I snore?"

I laughed and she followed suit.

She was having fun.

Union Station itself was magnificent, at least in structure. It looked like a cathedral, a renewal for travelers. But beneath vaulted ceiling and stained glass hid a mall. I took a pocketful of brochures about the place, and read them as I trailed Grace around. She went into every store, or so it seemed. Some she remained in long enough that I went outside and leaned against a railing, watching other shoppers, or sat on a bench, wondering how I came to be there. Staircases spiraled up to the next floor. Some shops had tinted windows, colored lights. Odd designs and mirrors gave the illusion of even more space and goods. Trinket vendors were the median in the breezeway, little walkways between their displays. We had coffee at a place with only three tall tables, the round top barely sufficient for our two cups. We propped our feet on metal bars circling the bottom. The station was designed for consumers on the move, to keep them consuming and keep them moving, ever looking. That was fine with Grace. She didn't want to alight until her eyes were already closing. No work *drew* her. No responsibility tasted as sweet as her leisure. Although she would never buy cheap jewelry, she lingered at the trinket vendors. Her interest caused sales clerks to stand near, to answer her questions. At one stand, where hundreds of bracelets and necklaces draped from round, wooden pegs, she slipped a gold chain free and laid it over the fingers of her left hand. "It should flow," she said, "ripple against skin. This is too heavy." She put it back, looked at a couple more pieces. The salesgirl, slim and feline, had countless chains on her neck and wrists. Of course they were cheap. The heavy traffic strip wasn't intended for the moneyed clientele. But there were rules to strolling a mall, games to play. We were in it together, weren't we? So said Grace's eyes, her clicking heels, her pert body and relentless energy. She could walk effortlessly, aimlessly, the movement itself reward sufficient for her and thus in her mind for me. I don't mind exercise, even exhaustion, for some *worthy* reason.

"Give in and have fun," she said. "Don't be a grump."

"I'm not much for shopping."

"You're a student of humanity," she said. "This is as good a sampling as any."

She slowly made our way to the far right end of the first level. There was the candy factory. Four young people were dressed in their own clothes but shared the common marking of a green apron and hat. They weren't smiling all the time, but they did pretty well. People were queued for service. Grace joined a line, swaying, gesturing me up beside her. "What shall we get?"

"You know I don't like candy."

"I do," she said. "And I want to hear them sing. It's not fair to wait and listen if we're not going to buy."

That was, of course, correct, but I didn't want to hear them sing, and especially to wait around, gawking, waiting for them to gratify the onlookers. They might wait for a long time, or not sing at all, or be terribly bad at it, and embarrass themselves and everyone watching. Grace wanted her candy and her song. She spoke to the woman in front of her. "Have you heard them?" The woman said "yes," she had, and they were very good, worth waiting on. Grace raised her fine eyebrows at me. See?

She bought three kinds of candy and had three small, rustling bags to carry. She handed them to me, but I hesitated long enough that she laughed and carried them herself.

The workers sang four times, and obviously enjoyed it.

"I told you," Grace said. "I'll bet they have to be able to sing to get the job. Anybody can make fudge. It's not demeaning, either. They wouldn't have taken the job if they didn't want it."

"I didn't say it was demeaning."

"No, you didn't." She took my arm. "You didn't have to."

She dragged me to a street artist's booth.

"Let me draw you separately," the fellow said. "Same price, unless you prefer to be drawn together."

Grace looked at me for the decision. "Separate?"

I nodded, and then saw her disappointment. Why did she offer the wrong choice first?

She sat down. He didn't even feign interest in her. He gave her big eyes, heavy short hair, chipmunk cheeks, and a tiny chin and tiny mouth. When he held the sketch up, finished, not really ask-

ing approval, she said, "Oh," plaintively and looked to me for re-
assurance. "Tell me, dear heart," with false levity, "that I don't look
like that."

"You don't," I said, and hoped she wouldn't say more. He wasn't
there because he was talented. He was there because he could support himself.

She turned to view the displays hanging behind his booth. They
weren't too good, most of them unflattering in some way, and a few
very ugly. The people, though, could have come from one family.
The artist had a stock of features, mouths, cheeks, chins, eyes, and
hair, and simply matched them up differently.

"I can do another for you," the artist said to Grace.

"No, thanks. Once warned, twice shy, as they say." She handed
him the sketch and he rolled it up, put it in a tube for her, and motioned me toward the seat.

I didn't want to have myself drawn. What chance was there for
a decent portrait? But Grace insisted.

"Don't be so vain," she said.

He gave me a big chin, thinning hair, but eyes that may have
looked like mine. Grace said they did. "He was kinder to you than
to me," she said, where he could hear her.

She wanted to keep the sketches and I was glad enough of that.

"Do you plan to burn them?" I asked.

"Of course not!" A few feet on, stopping to find a particular
piece of fudge in one of the crinkled bags, she said, "Would you
have burned them, Arthur?"

"Why would you ask that?"

"Your tone, I guess. You really don't like them."

"Do you?"

"No," swinging off again, eyes still on me, though. "But they matter to me, anyhow."

When she became enamored with a dress shop, I watched the caricaturist sketch another customer. He liked having an audience and I wanted to soften Grace's barb.

Grace and I had a brief rest in our room, or she did, while I read the brochures provided by the management. Then to a restaurant of fine food, wine, service. I contributed the history of the station. "See?" Grace said again, "What you've gained from the trip? You not only know what it looks like, but the whole history."

"It's far from the entire history."

She knew that. She was sparkling.

She wouldn't sleep. She said she couldn't. When she finally lay down and let me turn out the lights, she drifted off. The silence and stillness were welcome but insufficient. I felt panic waiting, creeping around the room. I slipped from the bed and sat in the east chair against the wall. I focused my thoughts on my own apartment in Mason. It was no more than a cubbyhole, but it was always quiet there, and work was all around me, on the desk, in the closet, in my briefcase. In me. I could turn myself to something fruitful any time of the day and night. I could read the various revisions of *Ghosts*, to see if I had forgotten how to do something and needed to copy it from myself.

I wanted to be home. Without Grace. Without anyone.

⌒

A man might feel a quickening and have to slow it down. He might have to keep a lid on it. He has to look at a steady spot on the wall or out the window or get up and go outside and down the stairs and sit in the stairwell. If he opens and closes the door, there's a whooshing sound that can soothe him for a while. He can walk down all the flights, and come back up and enter the room very quietly, and feel that quickening again, as though he hadn't left at all. And there she lies on the bed, on her back, little bird face straight up, hands drawn close to her shoulders, palms to the ceiling. Palms to the ceiling. It could be a game.

So he sits in a chair. A light of some kind blinks through the window across the wall and out the other window, though that's not possible. Is it? For light to come and go on its own like that?

One day and night gone but lasting too long still. And there she lies, resting for the morrow, for another long passage of nothing fun. Arthur this. Arthur that. Arthur. While on her back she lies. He comes to the bed and bends down to see who exactly is lying there. Is that his mother? No. Of course not his mother. He puts one hand scant inches above her parted lips. He can feel her life in his own palm, very faint, a weak little life. She might wake and say something wrong, something ugly or stupid or just something. He waits for her to do that. He remembers having to stand still for so long his body hurt. Her eyelids flicker so he knows she's awake, somewhere she's awake and she knows who's standing here and what he's about. But she doesn't open her eyes. Won't. She'll let it be a dream. He knows they do that. They pretend to be sleeping beauties. She knows her car is in another city and no one in the world knows where she is, so she's not going to open her eyes. She'll dream on. She'll dream he's loving the very sight of her. He may lower his hand over that mouth, see the startle of silent fear, the O O O. Something happens. A moan or subtle turn. A door shut. A laugh. A light blinking through the window. A scream out in the street.

He lifts his dead hand with the other, and cradles it like a wound. He goes back to the chair and spends the night there. He doesn't sleep because he has to stay awake in case something happens or has to happen or has to be stopped from happening. When she wakes in the morning, all muss and puffiness, she averts her eyes, and so he knows for certain that she knows, though she may not admit it yet.

"I must look a sight," she says. "I had a rough night."

⟶

Grace was quieter on the return home. We both read. She still had a bag of candy, but kept it on the side away from me. She took pieces out very slowly and when they were all consumed, she folded the bag into a small square, wrapped it in a tissue and put it in the magazine carrier before her. She had had fun. She was thoroughly exhausted, but she could catch up. She took my hand once between her own and patted it. It was an unusual gesture from her, very old-fashioned and motherly. "Thank you," she said. "I know how much you didn't want to go."

She slept off and on. I thought perhaps that, too, was a pretense, so we could continue forever.

I've never understood them, any of them. They wait and wait, all hungry for you. Why don't they just gobble you up and be done with it?

⟶

I saw an interview with a serial killer. He said he wished someone would tell him why he did the things he did. He described picking up a prostitute, driving with her in the front seat, then just hitting her in the head with a hammer, dropping it, and choking her.

"You didn't know you were going to kill her?" the interviewer asked.

"Hunh-uh. I just knew I was doing it."

He wasn't a bright man. He was like an animal with a voice. He may have been telling the truth.

One intended victim described a change in the killer's features and voice. The killer had become like another person entirely, a different cast in his eyes. I think the poor devil probably was observing as much as the victim was, and wanted to wrench himself out of this world altogether.

—

On Christmas morning, at 8:00 a.m., Grace called me from Jackson, Mississippi. "I just wanted to wish you Merry Christmas before anyone else does."

"You succeeded. No one's likely to call me but you."

"Then you can get all that work done, right?"

"Not all of it, but a good inroad."

She was concerned about me. I heard caution in her voice. "You should leave it all alone a while, Arthur, even if you stay there. Do you have some family or friends to visit? You have time. There's almost a week left. Do something you really want to do."

"I am. This is it. You forget that I wanted to come to Mason and I want to stay."

"Right. Well," she said, "then I'll let you get to it. I don't suppose you miss me?"

"I miss you."

The silence was unreadable. Then she decided. "Good. I hope that feeling, sir, continues to grow."

The phone clicked.

I couldn't go back to sleep. I couldn't rest. I was alone, agitated. Grace had stirred up that loneliness. I had no place to go, that was true. Sometimes nothing that is common to you will satisfy the urge that wells within you. You would squelch it with anything in your power. I wandered into the kitchen, fixed coffee, went into the living room. I was fifty years old, living in Mason, Missouri, during the holidays, in an almost-empty, huge house. I felt homesick, nostalgic, hungry, hurt. I tried writing. I went down to the common lounge. Came back. Tried reading. Lifted weights. Lay back on the floor and stared at the ceiling. I had to get out of myself. I knew that. I was wallowing in self-pity without even knowing what I pitied myself for. For not having been something significant.

So, I looked up Nada Petrovich in the student directory. It was a rural route, one where direction meets direction, SE 140, #444. I drove out there. By then it was just after noon. A low, winter-hazed sun, crisp, still air. I had been invited, so I guess I could have just driven straight to her house, banged on the door. But I didn't want to intrude. What if they were right in the middle of dinner? What if the house were full of people, all of whom I didn't know? What if her "gentleman friend" and she were in the midst of an intimate moment? Not likely, but I didn't want to cause any awkwardness.

I could see the house from the highway, a small white frame house at the end of a dirt road, about a mile and half away. Only one car was parked in front, but she could have picked her friend up at the airport. I backtracked to another dirt road, parked, and walked across the fields to Nada's. Anyone could have seen me. I even thought Nada might see me coming, or sense it with that uncanny way she had, but she didn't. I thought, too, that her house would *look* Christmasy—a wreath on the door, candles in the windows, wood piled on the porch. Maybe smoke rising. But it didn't. Stark, lonesome little house. I didn't knock, but I did stand by the wooden porch, listening. Along its edge were empty flower beds, filled with uncleared stubble that could have been from the year before, and edged by white stones of various sizes. They were unusual, with the vapory opaqueness of opals. When she didn't appear, I walked around the house and glanced through the windows. I remember the grass was dead and dry enough to crackle. The sides and back of the house were braced with stone blocks, with no underpinning. One could easily crawl beneath the house its entire length. Old houses are often made like that, allowing for rising water in wet years and for cool breezes in hot, dry ones.

I passed what appeared to be a study with a desk and bookcases, the latter filled with blue canvas notebooks; on to a small bedroom, then a larger bedroom with a four-poster bed, a wardrobe, and quilt holder. Past the bed, beside a dresser, a doorway gave to the rest of the house, and at the far end of a distant room, I saw Nada, seated and lifting a glass in a toast toward the other end of the table, which was out of sight. I couldn't see the gentleman himself, so I walked on around the back porch, past high windows—probably the kitchen—and approached another, larger window that I assumed gave onto the dining room. Because I was on the south side of the house, I risked having my shadow fall over the table, but I wasn't doing anything anyhow. I'd just gesture hello and let myself be invited in.

But my shadow was small and fell behind Nada. And there wasn't anyone at the other end of the table who could see me. She was alone. Drinking a toast to an empty room or to a table full of food. She was dressed in red velvet that revealed her shoulders and upper back, humpy, white, and as bare as a baby's buttocks. Her raised arm was a drape of scalloped fat. I immediately squatted down. I couldn't go in then, could I? I don't think I was totally surprised. Maybe I'd had suspicions all along and they were confirmed so simply and suddenly that I was momentarily taken aback. I crawled under the house, because it was so easy to do. I was immediately out of sight if someone *did* look. If a man had just been out of the room, I would hear him walking, or hear his voice. Something. I was right under the dining room, though, and no one was there. I heard *her* get up and go toward the front. Then I heard the front door open, in seconds close. She went back to the dining room and stood quietly. Then she went back to the front door again. She knew something. She really had a gift.

Or she had seen me.

She might have seen my reflection in her wine glass. If so, she knew I was somewhere about the place. I listened intently. If she came looking, came outside, I would know. I could be ready. Her movements inside the house were obvious. The weight of her creaked the boards and even her hesitations I could visualize. I was fairly sure she was alone, but someone *could* have been in there. Any one viewpoint is limited, and even mirrors leave hidden angles. I waited. It wasn't too chilly and there was a timelessness about the situation, like an old story with a child waiting on presents above, waiting maybe on a top, on something to spin, spin. When she had not moved for a long time, I suspected she slept, which old women often do. I crawled to the other side of the house, out, and then sped across the yard, down the sloping north field, and circled back to my car.

In the early evening, I phoned her. "Merry Christmas," I said.

"Dr. Blume?"

"Mister Blume. Remember? I just wanted to wish you Happy Holidays. I hope your guest made it."

I could sense her thinking, almost see her blue, crafty eyes. "More people came than I expected," she said.

See?

That was my first genuine clue that Nada wasn't exactly what I thought she was. I couldn't picture her in the old way anymore and I missed the fondness I had felt for her. I pitied her, though. She still had rights.

―

The rest of Christmas break, I tried to begin a new manuscript, to explore the mind of a woman like Nada. Now, there was a twisting and turning, a stop-short and can't-go-on.

On January third, the phone rang, but I didn't answer it. It had to be Grace, returned from Jackson, and I hadn't yet bought her a gift. That was inexcusable of me. I could cover myself easily enough—the next morning I'd run to the bookstore and get her a good edition of some woman's wit, like Edna St. Vincent Millay, Dorothy Parker, maybe some softer work like Browning. I know how to please women even on short notice.

But mostly I didn't answer because I was really ill—chills, fever, nausea, burning eyes, and lethargy. It was that stone lethargy that comes from trying to write what you can't understand.

CHAPTER 16

There's this species of beetle that lays many eggs when the food supply is plentiful. But when food's sparse, the female will produce only one egg, which remains attached to the exterior of her body. When the larva emerges, it gradually consumes the mother's body. Sickening, isn't it? Yet it sounds like self-sacrifice. Whatever it is, it's natural.

My mother and I never discussed her illness, at least not directly. She'd apologize to me sometimes for not being a "normal mother," but she was referring to the wild fancies that beset her for days, the frenzies that racked her and actually hurt her worse than they did me. She'd forget to eat, be unable to sleep, as if she were scaling castle walls or fighting witches and demons, or saving Christ—one of her dominant delusions—from the pit. She'd have injuries, scratches, and cuts. Once she came home at dawn, still dressed in her nightgown. It was ripped, mud-streaked, and bloody from her hands. Two of her fingernails were ripped loose to the quick, the others torn ragged. "I couldn't get him out," she said. I never did learn where she had been digging, but it had to have been rocky.

⌐

She liked white cotton nightgowns. I suspect that came from either her childhood or from her reading. I bought her one for Christmas every now and then.

⌐

She liked holidays, and did pretty well. I wasn't actually deprived. We did the old-fashioned kind of decorations. We strung popcorn and cranberries. We made angels of cornhusks and clothespins. She usually made divinity candy, tied the pieces in waxed paper, and hung them from the tree with red thread. It wasn't much, but it was wonderful in its own way. Once I painted her likeness—as best I could—on a wooden shim. She put it on the top of the tree. She burned that image the next July. She made a little mound of dirt at the edge of the garden, shredded paper in the center, covered it with broken twigs, and placed the shim on the twigs. She lit the paper and sat on her haunches while the little fire blazed.

Every Christmas I got new clothes—three complete sets of underwear, shirts, and jeans or slacks. Sometimes a jacket or gloves. I got the same on my birthday, too, and when school began in the fall. I never had to be ashamed of my clothing. But I also got real gifts. She tried to do right by me. I got books, of course, always, from some unending list she had. And always a special gift, a little joy. A harmonica—I never learned to play it, but I could blow a fierce cacophony of moods. Slingshot with steel pellets. A World War II helmet. Bow and arrow. Fishing rod and reel. Bayonet. BB gun. Knife. Bowie knife. Saber. Binoculars. Camera—she wouldn't let me take her picture. I tried to catch her sleeping. She woke up.

"I'll throw it away," she said.

Once she gave me a small wooden box, hand-carved, probably from India. Inside were a few snapshots of herself as a young girl, of my grandparents. One of Mr. Sutton on our front porch. He was seated on the step, partly in shadow, smiling. He looked happy and lighthearted, not at all as I remembered him. And one photograph of a man I didn't know. He was young, tall, and lean, wearing overalls with no shirt, and—incongruously with the overalls—a floppy-brimmed dark hat.

"Who's this?" I asked. She was watching me.

"He stayed in the hunters' cabin for a while."

"What's his name?"

"Tim Welker."

"Why do you have a picture of him?"

"Oh, guess I thought he was good-looking."

"Where's he at now?"

She didn't answer.

Those pictures disappeared sometime while I was in Wilshire. She left the box, though. She filled it with pills. I wanted to see the photos again and she probably knew that. I suppose it didn't matter much who my father was, since I was *her* son.

⌒

Her bedroom was off the living room. She'd leave her door open or come stand in it.

⌒

I applied for every scholarship and award, and I aced my way through the undergraduate program at Wilshire. All the while, I worked twenty-five hours a week at Buford's Pharmacy, serving as stock and delivery boy, clerk, and all-around janitor. I was good at my job, never complained, never asked for a raise. I continued working there through graduate studies, when I was also a graduate assistant. I wasn't as comfortable with Buford as with Mr. Watson. The latter knew my mother and her family, and I had around me a sense of community and history, of place, even if the place was low. To Buford, I was a series of functions.

My time was totally consumed, but it was for the future, a future.

I sent or took money to my mother all the years I was in school and for a long time after. At first, it was a pittance, but it increased as my earnings did. That may not sound like much, but I thought it was. I believed she *needed* my help.

⌒

Fathers was published my last year in graduate school. I was almost thirty and my mother forty-seven. I called her from Wilshire. She didn't understand the hoopla about national contests, readings, and so on, but she was glad for me.

"Did you win any money?" she asked.

"A little. Five hundred dollars. But they're *publishing* it. That's the thing."

Her idea of success was money, but how could she know any different? That's what bought her the little freedom and comfort she could have. She had never worked. She had never been sane long enough to follow a line of development from beginning to logical end.

"I'll be reading in Baton Rouge, before the creative writing students and teachers. I'm the featured writer."

That had no meaning to her. She wouldn't come to the reading because "Baton Rouge might as well be China." It was too far away for her in many ways. If she had become frenzied, where could she have gone? She wouldn't have trusted me to save her.

Actually, I was sort of glad she wouldn't come. I had made it, slipped over the top where oddball becomes artist and ugly becomes beauty. That was my heyday, idyll, golden era. Boom, explosion into PROMISING. I need never doubt myself again.

⟿

The award ceremony was held in a small, tasteful auditorium designed for such events. The upholstered seats were wide, with adequate passage room. Two aisles divided the curving rows. Above, not used that night, were three small balconies, disconnected and private, for important families or select groups. The furnishings were rich wood, red and deep blue and gold draperies and carpets. A long red rug cushioned steps to and from the platform podium. The microphone was so sensitive that the announcer's words were couched in a sound like a long exhalation. It was as much sanctuary as stage.

After the reading, we writers beset the town. I was the young crowd's guest at their favorite hangout. The tables were round, small, and completely movable. My hosts drew together empty tables, random empty chairs, and we overtook the space around one of the pool tables in the back. Someone was at my table the entire evening. They regaled me with novel plots and characters and queried me about my own methods. What was my writing routine? Did I write in the morning or evening? Did I compose in longhand or by typewriter?

"Longhand," I told them, and shared the well-known tale of Faulkner's having written *As I Lay Dying* while he worked as a night watchman, taking only six weeks to complete the masterpiece and using as paper only napkins. "He wrote another novel," I said, "on the wallpaper of a room."

Such are the hors d'oeuvres of writer gatherings. Whether or not they're true doesn't matter, just that they're interesting and the person who stated them was worth attending.

Some of the student writers played pool, even the young girls, and I wondered what it would be like to stay there. To retain their admiration. The young men treated the girls casually. One girl bent over the table to sight down the cue stick and a player nearby pretended to pat her behind, while another, by me, pushed his cue stick down her top, between her breasts. She didn't jerk or squeal or flash indignation. The fellows whooped. She took her shot. I don't recall if she made it. When she came around the table for another shot, I saw that her skirt barely covered the curve of her lower buttocks. It was an intricate display and claim and I wondered, if I lived among them long enough, what I might do. The girl let her eyes linger on me a few times, but I didn't warrant breaking up the game or more than a forgettable greeting. There were other girls there, but I've forgotten what they looked like. Accompanying wraiths. Even then I knew that high regard wanes quickly and I hadn't attained but a rung on the ladder. After such award gatherings or conferences, the writing community buzzes with the pranks of the elite, the stories that will be legends about the formative years of the famous.

Arthur J. Blume was a nice guy. I imagine they reported that. He stayed with them until the bar closed and he probably went home with one of the girls. Which one? They might have conjectured, given me a bit of the old goat touch. Actually, he stayed with the group until it began to disperse naturally, then went to his room so he would not be left alone. He sat on his bed and recalled every bit of praise about his book. He read to himself the same passage he had read to the audience. It moved him to tears, which he thought was egotistical. He wanted to move *other* people to tears, not himself.

⟵

In December, I took copies of the book home. Through the kitchen window the winter sun came lazy and oddly warm. The curtains were yellow and perhaps the warmth came from those—from memory more than fact. She wore a dress with no belt. It was dark blue, splotched with disembodied lavender blossoms, no stems or leaves. Her arms were still slender, but the flesh hung slightly, from the elbow to wrist. I knew that hadn't always been so, but I didn't know when the change had occurred. I had been home at least once a month for years.

"Are you well?"

"Do I look sick?"

"I don't know."

"I'm well enough," she said.

That afternoon she read my book in one sitting, in her easy chair by the front double windows. Outside, a wind picked up, and the sun disappeared into the winter sky. She read slowly.

When she finished, she closed the book. "I thought there'd be more to it," she said. "Since it won a contest."

"Like what? Like what more?"

"I wanted to like it, Arthur, but I don't know what it's about. What is it about?"

"It's two young men attempting to discover their fathers. Who their fathers were."

"Just by talking?"

"I don't mean who they were physically. What they were really like. It's about the boys' dreams, their hopes."

She turned the book over and looked at my photograph. Then she placed the book on the coffee table. "I'm sorry," she said. She rose. "But you're happy now it's published?"

"Yes. Yes, I am."

"Then that's good enough."

She wanted me to take a copy to my old employer, David Watson, and to give one to the library. I did both. Mr. Watson wanted to buy extras, but I wanted to keep the few I had. "You could order more from a bookstore," I said. "That would go on record as a real sale. I mean, I get royalties from that kind of sale."

"I'll do that," he said. He asked me to sign his copy. "I knew you were a special kid, Arthur," he said. "So quiet. I used to worry about you. Guess I didn't have to."

He really was a good man. He did what he could.

That evening, I was uncertain how to behave at home. The book should have changed things. I knew that. I felt it. I wanted it. But life goes on and on about the same.

Once she seemed to have chilled, and she stood on the furnace floor-grating.

"I hate winter," she said.

"I do, too."

When she retired, I continued reading. I was aware of the light beneath her door. When it turned black, I waited. Just as I turned off the lamp by my chair, I heard her door open.

⌒

I read that sounds may drive a mild creature to frenzy. Domestic dogs that live with a family from childhood, care for the human young, guard against strangers and other mishaps, suddenly turn and kill the very being they have protected. The sounds suspected were of a creaking gate, a swing, a high whining motor, a drill. The actual sounds involved are likely far more numerous. Everywhere in the world something is walking around fine-tuned for a frequency all its own.

⌒

I have favorite books: *Les Miserables, The Hunchback of Notre Dame, The Three Musketeers, A Tale of Two Cities, Remembrance of Things Past, The Sun Also Rises, King Lear, Othello, The Possessed, The Idiot, The Castle of Otranto, Tom Jones, The Turn of the Screw, Of Mice and Men, Don Quixote.* And *The Four Feathers.* A despicable man tries to redeem himself in secret. He risks his life many times over to undo a past shame. A person's motives must matter and a whole life should count more than only pivotal moments.

CHAPTER 17

I saw televised segments of the trial of two men who had teamed
up for capture and torture. One of them was plagued with his
own horror. He was tall and bearded and bent, like something
handsome that got twisted. The other was a plague himself. They
took girls to a cabin and filmed what they did to them. One scene
flashed on the screen, of a girl tied to a chair, blindfolded, screaming, nude. Bloody. I fled the room. The one monster managed to
kill himself before the trial ended. The other still lives on at our
expense.

How could I be evil and not know it, since I recognize it when
I see it?

⟶

Grace brought Nada a brooch, an opal surrounded by red stones.
"They're rubies," Nada explained. "Dr. Burch got it at an estate
sale. She got Margaret jewelry, too, but not as nice as this. She always gives us gift certificates, but not this year."

I asked Grace why she would give Margaret anything, even at
Christmas. She reminded me that Margaret had forty bosses. "I

gave her a stick pin," she said, conspiratorially. "Surely you appreciate that. Women wear them now, like brooches."

———

Grace wanted to be with me. Who knows why? Many of them have, and some of them were good women. One ironed shirts for me. She said it soothed her. I graded papers with an instructor who couldn't write notes in pen because they were always too harsh or too lenient and she refined them and ended up raising grades to make life easy for herself and her students. There was a professor's wife who had two children. He left her and she cried often. She liked hot chocolate and rain. They were intelligent women, not always attractive, too effacing perhaps. Some small thing went awry and one of us moved on, usually me. They gave me no reason to expect to see them again.

Grace was always after something. Maybe she liked the risk of me.

———

That first day back, after Christmas break, Dr. Walsh saw me at the mailboxes and waved me in to his office. Margaret, safe in her vinyl chastity partition, watched me pass. Walsh closed the door behind us.

"How was your holiday?" he asked. "Did you go anywhere special?"

"I like to stay close to home at Christmas. It's a good time to burrow in and concentrate."

"New book, huh?"

"Yes."

His desk was positioned in a corner between two windows, and I had already seen the long tube lying on one window ledge. Walsh took it up, surreptitiously eyeing me as he did so. "I wanted to ask you about this." With one finger he twisted the white sheet into a tighter curl and withdrew it from the tube. "You know anything about it?"

"About what?"

He rolled the sheet out and there was a particularly good caricature of a hefty woman with porcine cheeks and nose.

"What is it?" I said.

"It was sent to Margaret."

"For what purpose?"

"That's what I'm asking you."

"You're suggesting, I guess," I said, "that I sent it to her." I stood up. "I don't understand the kind of weight she carries here. She seems to take a dislike to certain people, like me, and go out of her way to cause them trouble. I think she hopes to damage your opinion of me, and I'm sorry about that. But I don't want to take part in this kind of discussion unless it's absolutely necessary. Maybe you should ask her to come in and see if she'll charge me to my face."

He was visibly interpreting me. He was an intelligent man, and diplomatic, rather deceptively naïve. He didn't trust me. But he had to know the type of woman who was serving as his secretary, and he had to be slightly ashamed about that. He might have been grateful to me.

"Sorry," he said. He rolled the picture up and inserted it back in the tube. He returned it to the window ledge. "I'm not going to ask her in because it will just exacerbate the matter. I know you're right. And I do apologize. I'm not even sure the thing was sent as an insult, although it's odd there was no return address."

"Where was it postmarked?"

"St. Louis, I think. The print's so faint. You didn't go there, you say, but someone else probably did. They may have sent this thing as a Christmas gift and we'll hear about it later. It might be a little awkward for Margaret," he caught himself, "and for the other person, too. Sorry, Arthur. It's all part of my job."

"I understand. Don't think twice about it." I asked about his holiday, as he had mine. When I left the office I saw Margaret's unveiled interest in my expression, my possible embarrassment. I was tempted to wink at her, a simple little human gesture. But self-preservation told me to keep my face perfectly impassive.

She scampered from her place before I even rounded the corner.

Margaret lived in one of the newer, less expensive housing developments. Her lot was on a cul-de-sac, with two houses on either side of her. Most of the land around it had been cleared and scraped for the erection of more tract houses, but a few copses had temporarily survived, and one of them was host to a mistletoe. I broke off a couple of twigs heavy with berries and placed them at her front door.

This was innocuous, not even kind for kind, much less degree for degree. People should have to be afraid of retribution.

⟶

It had never occurred to me that Nada could actually enroll in the advanced creative writing class. But the old miss had aced the prerequisite long before I appeared at Mason, and, as she announced to the entire class, she had "been published many, many times." She added, "Publication is more important than formal education in writing, anyhow. Isn't it, Professor Blume?"

"That depends."

She had brought evidence of her own success—two leather-bound volumes and a stack of thin, saddle-stapled publications. "I have a poem in each of these," she said. She held up one of the shabbier, paper journals. It was the kind known in our trade as a "toilet paper journal," constructed of letter-sized paper folded and stapled across the middle. The pages appeared crammed with single-spaced poetry and prose. The cover was of slightly heavier bond, lavender, with the title *Heirlooms* in heavy, crude calligraphy. She tapped it. "And *five* in this one." She addressed her classmates. "You should send your work out. Really."

She sat down in the seat she had chosen, directly to my right. She didn't want to be *just* a student.

I wanted to advise the class that such publications were a liability to the writer, not a credit. But I couldn't. To correct her would have embarrassed both of us.

"When you feel ready," I told them, "do submit your work. But research the market first. Decide your own goals. And, please, address me as Mr. Blume. Professor Blume is not actually correct, and I prefer 'Mister' in any case."

She pouted a little. I had disappointed her.

During break, I saw amiable Billy Butler examining the journals and jotting down some addresses. Jack was observing. After class, I detained the boys long enough to explain how the journals did business. "The writers actually pay for the publication," I said. "They pay a submission fee of a dollar or more a poem. The editors will select one piece from a person who submitted, say, twenty poems. That ensures the person will likely submit again. Quality doesn't matter. Money does. They can run enough copies for the authors and pocket some cash. As for the nicer books, they cost a pretty penny. I imagine Nada paid fifty or seventy-five dollars for each of the leather-bound volumes. The authors—or their friends and family—buy the books. No one else would. The writers are paying to be published, whether they believe it or not."

Jack was studying me.

"No, young man," I said. "I had more sense even as a young writer."

"Are you going to tell Nada about it?"

"No. It'd be taking away everything she bases her talent on."

He considered the answer, accepted it. "Right. Why'd you tell us?"

"Because your work deserves better."

"Mine, too?" from Billy.

"Yours, too."

"What about the other students?" Jack said. "You going to warn them?"

"You and Billy can pass the word if you want to. Subtly."

I'm certain Jack understood that I was protecting Nada while guiding the other students. It was a delicate balance of responsibility.

Neither of them would tell Nada. Warning her would hurt her. Choices are difficult. It's easier just to let things happen.

⟵

I found a worn blue notebook on my desk. It had been carried and touched often. I lifted the top cover enough to see her name on the top right of a yellowed page.

She came looking for it that afternoon. "Did I leave my note-book in here?" she said.

I gestured toward the table beside her.

She picked the notebook up, peeked inside, then closed it. "Dr. Loeffle asked to see some of my poems," she said. "I told him I'm taking your class. I wondered where I left this."

"You knew exactly where you left it. I'm not going to read your work now, all right? You have to submit manuscripts as the other students do, in *turn*, on schedule."

"Oh, you," she protested. "A person makes a mistake and you get all ruffled about it. I don't even want you to read my poems. That's why I asked Dr. Loeffle. So I'd know which ones to submit to class. I want to choose my best ones."

"If that's really what you want, I'll help. I don't mind selecting the best of your pieces for class discussion. That's part of my job."

"I could help you, too, you know. I could grade the others' poems for misspellings and typos. I could make copies when you want them. I could. . . ."

I took her hand. She stopped talking. "I just want to get better," she said. "No one takes me seriously."

"I do."

She withdrew her hand and hugged the notebook. "I have *many* of these."

"All poems?"

No, she told me. Songs, letters, stories, thoughts, things that had happened to her. She'd been writing since she was a girl and she had saved every piece. She had rewritten them, neatly, organized them. Volumes and volumes.

"How old are you?"

"Seventy-three."

"You don't look it. You're a lovely, talented woman."

She tsked her way out the door.

What had she created, I wondered, between all those covers over all those years? Surely an entire lifetime couldn't be worth nothing at all.

↼

Carl Loeffle said yes, Nada had spoken with him. "I told her I'd be happy to read her stuff, but not now. Spring break would be a good time."

She had not exactly lied, then, just manipulated, to make me read her work when *she* wanted me to.

↼

"Oh," Grace said, and clapped her hands over her face as if she herself were shamed and excited simultaneously. "She's kept *diaries!* That's what they are. And you, Arthur, will have to read them all. There's no escape for you now." She laughed her little Tinker Bell laugh, kissed me, and scooted out of bed toward the shower.

"Have you read any of her writing?" I called.

"Papers. Just dry, dry papers. She loves authority and she patches in quotations like she's quilting. She's accurate." She peeked around the door frame. "But you know, she might be good in a genre. She has a kind of sappy appeal personally. If she could get that in writing, some people might like it."

Sound of shower. Dark bedroom. Streetlight filtering through drapes. Dark furniture. Grace reappearing with wet hair, sleeked back. White slender body. Gay voice.

"We never say sweet things to each other, Arthur."

I readied myself for a new request.

She sat on the bed, put her right hand on my chest, over my heart. She leaned to kiss my lips. I closed my eyes and she kissed my eyelids. In a moment, she sat up and I looked at her again.

"You have beautiful eyes," she said. "They're so sad."

Her voice was not at all sensual or playful. I wanted to fill the void between us so she might stay just as she was and not ask for more. I cupped my hand over hers. "The beautiful and sad are always joined." Nothing else would come from me. I felt her small anguish. "It's a pity," I said.

She moved her hand, arose. "Where in the hell are my cigarettes," she muttered and went into the bathroom.

I wanted to say the right thing. I followed her. She was looking in the mirror. I held her from behind, my forearms locked across her rib cage. I rocked her, buried my face in her thick, soft hair. When I drew back, she was watching our reflection. I didn't know what she saw. I didn't look at myself holding her, but released her and returned to bed. She didn't join me immediately. When she did, she sat beside me, looking down.

"What kind of woman do you like?" she said.

"Your kind."

"And have there been many of me?"

"None just like you."

She leaned over me, peering at my face. "I can't figure you out."

"I'm exactly what you see."

"No, you're more than that."

I kissed her and she stopped talking, laid her cheek on my shoulder. We remained like that for a while. I felt our hearts beat together.

She thought it was best if I didn't spend the night, so I dressed and went out in the cold night, trekking up to my car.

I had wanted to tell her she had the bones of a small bird, but I didn't know if she would like hearing that, so I kept it to myself.

She could arouse a great tenderness in me, but I couldn't sustain it. Maybe neither of us could.

⟵

Even songbirds noted for fidelity aren't faithful. Let a fellow sing his heart out and a strange female will dally with him and then dart back to her mate's nest. Maybe he knows and doesn't care.

⟵

Grace was good with students, in spite of using them as conversational fodder. One was often in her office, listening while Grace chatted away about authors and characters as if they had attended a tea at her house. She gestured a great deal. It made a good scene. She *looked* fond of them. I wanted to accept that she was, genuinely, but the belief eluded me. Her mocking words about students had to mean something, else why say them?

Of course, one can nurture without fondness, and be fond without nurturing.

⟵

Nada's notebook popped up again.

A snowstorm hit mid-afternoon, the whirling, blinding, ground-covering kind. Night classes were cancelled. I graded papers, worked out, napped, read, thought about my new book. Shortly after 6:00 that evening, someone knocked at my door. Jack Goff. I was *so* pleased. He thrust a blue notebook at me.

"Nada said to give this to you."

I didn't take it. "Is she downstairs?"

"She caught me coming in. She said maybe you'd read it since class was cancelled."

"She shouldn't have you run her errands. This puts pressure on both of us."

"Yeah. Well." He again thrust the book toward me. "I told her I'd drop it off."

I took it. I couldn't leave the kid in the middle. "Would you come in? I have coffee, beer."

"No, thanks." He looked over my shoulder briefly. "I've got to study."

"Sure? You needn't stay long."

"No," he said, without hesitation. He bobbed his head, turned away with easy, angular grace. Life called.

I went to my sitting room window and looked down at the grounds. I thought Nada might be standing under the globe lights waiting to urge me onward with a slight wave and a clomp, clomp away. She wasn't there. Nobody was. Just snow and wind, like one of those glass-domed snow scenes.

So, I looked at the book. She had won my attention. She had lovely handwriting—long, slim lines, very firm. Nothing irresolute about it. My mother's handwriting was crimped, as if she had a limit for each letter, and she boxed them down, marched them along the paper.

The poems weren't *good*. But they weren't bad. They were cutesy at times, too rhyming, sometimes abrasive and out of control. None was really okay as it was. She grappled for poems instead of letting them open up for her. But some of her lines I really liked:

That one-eyed cat he skinned, ruining marbles for all time.
Sleep I love, the half-death risk of it.
Death comes marching up, stubborn fellow.

I read the entire notebook. Then I put a note on the front: "I'm not going to read this. You have to follow the same rules as everyone else." I removed the note shortly. Sheer lying is an insult and it isn't my way.

⌒

"She didn't *drive* in that storm," Grace said. "Don't be foolish. She's working you, Arthur, for sympathy. Don't you know she sleeps in the lounge sometimes?"

We were in the lounge. The upper half of the north wall was window, a cold winter day on the other side. Inside, beneath the window were long, armless, leather sofas, end to end. "There?"

"When she wants or needs to be in town during bad weather, sure. Why not? It's comfortable enough, far better than most of the world has." She gestured a sweep of the room. "Sink, refrigerator, microwave, and—across the hall—a bathroom."

"And you people let this go on?"

"Wait a minute. What do you mean 'you people'? You're talking to me, remember? Grace? The woman you sleep with?"

"I mean the department sanctions this? You know she sleeps in the lounge?"

"We *ignore* it. That's not the same thing as sanctioning it or giving our permission, which would make us responsible for it, even legally responsible, probably, if she were to take ill, for example, or fall, or who knows what. No one actually sees her there.

She gets up early enough to be dressed and studying by the time Margaret arrives. Margaret has tried to catch her, but Nada has an uncanny ability to know when that might happen, and she's never been caught."

"Even by you?"

There was a slight hesitation, which I assumed had to do with the word "caught." Grace wasn't a shabby opponent.

"Even by me."

"You shouldn't allow it, though."

"What's the harm? If we acknowledge what she does, we have to stop her. It's easier this way."

"It's like she's a poor servant or bastard kin. Let her stay in your home if you really care about her safety and comfort."

Grace feigned horror. "Invite her in? You're totally delusional, Arthur. You need someone to protect you."

If she hadn't been jesting, I would have been touched.

Dr. Walsh came in then, with a smile to the both of us.

He was responsible for everyone. Grace. Nada. Margaret. He had balances to maintain.

⌒

Nada's first class submission was in mid-February.

The kids liked her poems:

Sarah didn't want to "pick poems to death."

Billy wanted to stand up and read one of them the way he heard it. He gave it a strong lilt, bouncy and full of life.

Jack said, "Sure the voice struggles, and the poems themselves struggle, but they're filled with passion. You have to feel them. That's what writing's all about."

"I just write the way I think," Nada said, blossoming like an overblown orchid. "Nothing fancy, just the way I see the world."

I told them they had been generous readers. Nada waited for me outside my office door.

"You didn't say much about my poems," she said.

"The class covered all the points pretty well. I don't want to undercut their analysis. You should value their opinions as much as mine."

"You *always* give your comments at the end. You didn't say anything."

"Be satisfied with what the group said. I don't agree with them and you won't want to hear it. Accept my silence as a kindness."

"You don't like my poems."

"Yes, I do. But, candidly, I find them a little too sentimental and predictable."

"I think they're beautiful. The class thinks they're beautiful. And I get them published, too."

I tried to be direct, honest, but not too hurtful. "If you don't want the truth, don't ask for it and don't submit yourself to it. Do you know what we in the profession call such open demand for praise?"

She was pouting.

"Female," I said. "We call it female."

"That's terrible."

"Yes, it is. But it's largely accurate."

"They're lovely poems," she said. "And *true*. And you know it." She stalked away, all rump and bustle.

The next day, she brought me a brass candle and cover, the top perforated to cast patterned shadows. She needed comforting.

"Your poems do show promise," I said. "I can even quote some of the lines, and that's good. They stayed with me."

"Do," she said. "Please quote them."

I did, just a few:

Young ladies, go lightly, sail all around the earth.
Oh hold those lovely faces proud. Your gentle ways gird the days.
Love this face, oh do. Strong-boned and lonely.

So I was honest with her about her writing; it just took me a while to get it all out.

⌒

I wondered why a group of young readers would rally around an old woman's work. I was proud of them for championing her, especially Jack. He understood the need to protect. We had that in common.

I was also worried that maybe I was blind to talent.

CHAPTER 18

My mother became ill at the beginning of my third year teaching at a small university in Texas. I had not been home for the summer because I was in the academic publish-or-perish situation, and needed peace in order to work. It's during the third year that superiors decide whether or not you are an "asset to the profession" and worthy of keeping. If you make it, two years down the road they give you tenure and you are a permanent member of their elite community.

To the associate and full professors, one book by a junior colleague meant little.

"You'll have to publish another major work pretty soon," one of them told me. "People may act as if you've plenty of time, but they don't mean it."

He had just published his fifth novel, about the meanderings of a young woman traveling through Egypt by train. He had taken such a ride when he was seventeen, he said. He advised me to try something quite different for my second book. "Show them your versatility," he said.

That was what I had intended to do anyway, but once he told me to do so, it became difficult. No one wants others to shape him, to determine his needs and efforts. I'd find myself reading my prose with his sensibilities, which probably weren't as good as my own. Now I expected myself not only to write well, but surprisingly. That's impossible—you can't try to surprise yourself. I kept getting in traps, thinking mazes that held me incompetent and miserable.

Shortly after that semester began, I received a call from a woman I didn't know, a Belle Wilson. "I'm a friend of your mother's," she said. "She's going to have surgery and I thought you might want to come home. She told me not to call, but she doesn't always know what's best for her."

"How do you know my mother?"

"Everybody in this area knows your mother. Who do you think takes care of her when you're not around?"

"What's wrong with her? How serious is this?"

"It's diagnostic surgery. They'll probably go in tomorrow. I think you should come home."

I don't know where she got her tone. Accusative. She had never met me.

There was no one for me to call who could accept this responsibility, even if I had wanted to shun it. Mr. Watson, perhaps, my old employer at IGA. But I couldn't place work or goals above my mother's needs. I had to go.

I advised the office of the emergency and told them I'd be back within two weeks or less. Feverish and fearful one moment, I was stoic the next and happily excited after that. The excitement was shameful, but I think perhaps it was normal—I didn't wish her dead or want her dead, but what if that happened anyhow, without any choice on my part? Cataclysmic changes can order whole new worlds, and who wouldn't be enticed by that? I drove straight through, stopping only to catnap in the front seat from time to time.

When I drove up to my mother's house, I knew it was empty. Tall, narrow, and bare, it seemed so long abandoned that the walls were caving in toward a vacuum. Only a pale webbing of white paint remained. The few trees near the house burned russet and gold, like fires circling an early death.

Inside, I called for her but expected no answer. The cool, shadowy rooms were orderly, no indication of a passionate rage. Just a farmhouse, slightly dusty, with dark heavy furniture. And many books, of course. But she was still in charge. I wasn't in the house and *free*, you understand. I wouldn't have been there at all except for her.

I fixed coffee. She kept dry eggshells in a can on the counter and I crumbled one into the coffee pot as she had always done and sat at the table alone. In a little while, composed and ready, I called the hospital at Morehead some fifty miles away.

Yes, they had Mary Blume. She was recuperating nicely. And yes, she could receive visitors.

"What kind of surgery did she have?"

"What relation are you to her?"

"I'm her son."

"We'll let her tell you."

⟵

Her hair was fastened at the nape of her neck, the remaining length roped against itself and pulled over her shoulder. She was smoky-eyed, thin. Her collarbones rounded out at the base of the throat, then dipped in just before the shoulders, their delicate wingspread evident beneath the straps of her white gown. She was, though ill and racked, lovely. Just a different kind of loveliness. Tragic.

"You just come home," she asked, "or did they call you?"

"A Belle Wilson called."

"I told her not to do that. Guess she listened."

"Who is she?"

"Nobody."

"She knew to call me."

"I do talk about you. She knows where you teach." She pushed up on one elbow, doubled the pillow, and lay back, pulling the thick braid over her shoulder.

"Do you want me to raise the bed?" I asked.

"Yes. Do that, please."

I turned the crank until she held up her hand, then pulled a metal chair near the bed. "This Belle Wilson. Who is she?"

"She and her husband bought the Sutton place. She found me in the road and got me home. I walked too far that day."

"What's wrong with you?"

"Nothing now."

"I can ask the doctor."

"I had a female problem. They fixed it."

"Why were you in the road?"

"Doesn't matter. I hemorrhaged. You need to know more?"

"No."

I knew what was wrong with her now. She was hollow.

At her house again, I cleaned. I polished even the sides of furniture. Everything shone, softened. I stripped her bed, carried the linen to the wringer washer in the basement. I filled it with a hose from the wall sink. A basket of dirty clothing sat near the washer, white items, but I didn't touch any of those things. They looked personal, with maybe more signs of her illness. I bleached the sheets, rinsed them twice, and hung them on the wire lines in back of the house. The sheets billowed and slapped in the bright fall sun. I drove into town, to Watson's store. Mr. Watson asked about my mother and we visited a short time, two men who liked each other. It was peaceful and pleasant and normal. I bought stocks of food. At home I fixed Jell-O with sliced apples and bananas, baked potatoes, a roast, and a hen, enough food to last us a week. Her training had paid off, as had my own nature. She needed me.

I was certain I could take care of her.

The nurse wanted her to take a wheelchair from her room to the car, but she wouldn't do it. She was proud. She walked, a little curved and trembly, but I gave her my arm.

In the car, she said, "I'll be fine, now. You can go on back to your job."

"I'll stay a while. You come first."

"I don't need any help."

"I know. I want to do this."

In a little while, she said, "You're a good son."

When we stopped at the drugstore for prescriptions, she said, "Get me some books, too."

"I won't know which ones you haven't read."

"Bring some out to the car. They'll let you."

I did so. She made her choices and I carried the lot inside, paid for the ones she wanted.

"Your mom's already read some of these," the clerk said. "I'm sure she's bought them before."

She began reading even before we were outside town. She stopped, though, when I turned from the main road. Beside us stretched the Sutton land and fences. She held the book in her lap, inserting her thumb to mark her place.

"Iva Sutton was real good to me."

"Both the Suttons were."

"I hate what happened to her."

I didn't answer. Farther on, we passed the area of fence where Mrs. Sutton died, and my mother said, "I've never hurt a living creature deliberately."

I didn't know what she wanted from me. I just said, "I know that."

She returned to her reading.

She had to have a series of treatments—six weeks of chemotherapy, six weeks of radiation, and another six weeks of chemotherapy. I couldn't leave. I called Texas and told them I wouldn't be coming back. Yes, it made me miserable in a way. But I was also proud to do what was expected of me.

Her hair thinned from the chemotherapy. The radiation weakened her. I had to help her to and from the car. At home, she stayed in bed, slept, and read. She vomited. She had muscle spasms so severe she asked me to strike her, to slap her thigh, her calf, wherever the muscles cramped fiercely and relentlessly. Sometimes she moaned. I would sit in the living room and hear that moan. But she didn't complain. And for everything I did, every little thing, she said, "Thank you, Arthur."

When I finally had to wash her clothing and returned it to her room, slipping the folded undergarments into the bureau, she closed her eyes. As I left, she murmured again, "Thank you, Arthur."

In spring, she insisted on putting out a garden. She wore a wide-brimmed white hat, and spent hours each day troweling up the soil, planting flowers and vegetables at random. When I joined her, she would point the trowel and name what she had planted there. I don't know why. She read most afternoons and evenings, as she always had.

But as the days lengthened and sunlight crept into the house, seeping from wall to floor, to far corner, receding, I became depressed. I couldn't write. Before long, I couldn't read, but would stare at the page, not even thinking, afraid to think, waiting on something to rise from the page and urge me to action. I didn't want to eat. I had returned to my old upstairs bedroom, having at first slept sitting in the chair in her bedroom, then moving to the sofa when I realized her illness was passing. I began to leave my bedroom only to use the bathroom and, when she insisted, to sit with her at the table, forcing down a bite or two when she nodded at my plate. I remained more and more upstairs. Panes of windows, uncurtained, circled the room. Multiple squares reflected shifting green and gold, summer coming on full and hot. I lay, and lay, and lay. Summer washed over me.

She wouldn't leave me alone. She wasn't an educated woman, wasn't sophisticated, but she was bright in many ways. She goaded me to get up and out.

"Arthur!" she'd call from the bottom of the stairs. "I need you to change a light."

"Arthur! Get up now. Get down here. What kind of creature sleeps all the time?"

Arthur. Arthur. Arthur.

One morning she appeared carrying a white enamel pail. I knew what it was. She placed it by my bed. "You can stay here. Close the door. Don't eat. Use this. But you'll have to empty it yourself. I'm not coming up here anymore."

She did, though. She must have worried and sought a solution, as humans do, and decided on one. She came upstairs later, held up one pill, and placed it on a small oak stand across the room. She checked until the pill was gone and placed another one there. Then, twice a day, one pill. Her own prescriptions. She handed them to me like you entice a timid beast. I came out.

I began preparing to leave. Through phone calls and letters, I arranged a few interviews, and I was hired for the fall, to teach at a small university in Arkansas. It wasn't quite as good as the Texas school had been, but it was good enough.

Late that summer, maybe in a beginning tide that sometimes swept her away, she appeared in her bedroom doorway once more, in her white gown. Her hair was fuller then, rich black and tumbling. But she didn't say my name or anything. She just looked at me. Eventually she let her gaze drift to the window. It was night. The window reflection caught both of us, slightly at an angle, with the glow of my reading lamp like a shadow moon.

I didn't move. Things change no matter what you want or what you do. She turned back to her room and closed the door.

CHAPTER 19

Sexual function does not require true desire. It can be a social ploy, evidencing dominance or submission. Sometimes it's a friendly gesture: We are the best of friends. Me? Aggressive? Here, I extend not just my monkey hand but my monkey self. It's also a physical response to a stimulus such as fear. One may confuse the two feelings, desire and fear, may, in fact, conflate them. I read of a movie in which a woman held a knife to a man's throat while she caressed his genitals, then had intercourse with him. Some critics acclaimed this as exploration of a rarely acknowledged event, the rape of a male by a female. Other critics claimed it impossible to rape a male since only his pleasure effected the requisite physical state.

Like most human beings, I'm capable of responding appropriately in any intimate relationship, if only I'm not miscued.

No one ever held a knife to me, but one woman wanted me to strike her across her breasts with the flat of my hand. I could do it. I just went somewhere else while I did that and watched us. I didn't tell her what I thought. She wanted her body to be a bruise. Helen Masters.

I don't want to be surprised by laughter or a face that changes.

⌒

Friends of Mason Library, thanks to Nada Petrovich, invited me to read before their select group on what turned out to be the nastiest day of the month. It wasn't particularly cold, but the wind whistled and whipped from late dawn to early dusk and drove damp chill to the bones, not the kind of weather to entice an audience in Mason.

Grace planned to attend, but in her preoccupation with convention didn't want to ride with me. She had yet to attend any local function in my company.

"You should just be the author," she had said in the lounge. "Take your due. Be the guest who is unattached and therefore available to all those old dears. They'll be so happy they'll search out every piece you've ever written. Do you have copies of *Fathers* to sell?"

I told her "No," though of course I had a few put back. "I'll be reading from the new book, and they're not likely to find that anywhere."

"They will someday. Anyhow," she was back to her own arrival problem. "I'll come by myself or give some of the others a ride. Harper's coming. Maybe Walsh, too."

"I'd rather they didn't."

"That's not true. You'll enjoy having some colleagues there."

She was at ease gently calling me a liar. It's a difficult skill to acquire, defending one's interpretation of what is and is not true. "Am I allowed to reserve a front row seat for you," I asked, "or is that too overt?"

"Have I really been that bad?"

"I didn't say anything about good or bad."

"Right." She thought it over. "Just leave a book on one of the front chairs. If someone moves it, I'll shift for myself. It's not likely to be standing-room only, anyhow, not because of you, but because of Mason and the lovely, lovely weather, which has cooperated as usual."

I wasn't angry, even irritated, but I no longer wished to save her a chair and didn't relish the idea of her being there at all. She had managed to denigrate the event. It wasn't much, I know—nothing that would add luster to a vita. It could at best, professionally, be listed as a reading, with the hope that no one knew the true nature of Mason's Friends of the Library. But they had invited me with a formal invitation, written by hand on an ivory card and actually posted. I had accepted first by phone and then by a similar note. I had read before similar groups. The women would come in nice dresses or suits; maybe a few would wear dress slacks. They would be polished, spiff, their very attire part of their respect for me. They had put a nice little article in the paper about it, including the time and place, and that I would read from my "new novel." It was an artful evasion, intended to compliment the writer.

Grace had said a few colleagues might come. That too, I could have lived without hearing. Let them come or not, but don't predict the *failure* so it can be endured twice.

I didn't try to reserve a seat. There were about twenty chairs and only five or so occupied. I sat on the front row by myself, waiting for someone to take charge. One of the hostesses brought me a glass of water and a napkin. "Nada wonders if you would like some fruit punch now, before the reading."

"No, thank you," I said, and half turned to acknowledge Nada with a nod.

I relaxed when I heard people entering, the shuffling of feet and the soft clunk of folding chairs being adjusted. I felt a touch on my back and expected it to be Grace.

The voice was Justinia's. "Hi, Bloomin' Arthur. Just learned about this at the Union."

I turned to greet her. Her blonde hair was wild, her eyes drowsy brown.

"Surprised you, didn't I?" she said.

"I told my students they shouldn't bother coming."

"That's what Jack said, but then I'm not your student, am I? I told Jack he should get his ass over here anyhow. So should Sarah the princess and the others."

"I don't require my classes to serve as audience."

"You should. That's what teachers do. Just give them extra credit, let it replace an exam. You know, tit for tat. If they don't come, take some points off their grade."

"Sit here," I said. "And look entertained."

Grace arrived late, as I was standing by the podium during the introduction. She was bundled for a blizzard. She wore black wool slacks, stylishly loose, topped with a bulky red and black sweater. Her shoes were loafers, and the socks on her tiny feet were also black. But on Grace, black was most becoming. I suppose black is becoming to most women. She raised her hands at the filled rows— what could she do? She could have come on time. Nada brought over a folding chair from the refreshment table, but Grace declined it and stood.

Moments into the reading, Carl Loeffle and Paul Harper entered, though apparently they hadn't come together. Loeffle mimed an apology, and stood by Grace. Harper sauntered over to the refreshment table, dropped his rucksack to his feet, took a handful of cookies, and turned around to listen.

I began again, explaining the premise of *Ghosts.* Then I read one complete chapter. Every now and then someone would nod assertively. Older audiences always do that and I don't know what it means—do they agree? Is it a particularly good passage? Have they heard a similar one before? Years ago there must have been an accepted etiquette for audience behavior, and one requirement was to nod occasionally. I have been tempted to stop abruptly and to ask a nodder to repeat, verbatim or in paraphrase, what I had just read.

Justinia swung one foot the entire time; she also pushed back the cuticles on each of her red fingernails.

The applause seemed genuine. It was very much appreciated.

When I stepped down, Carl Loeffle hurried forward. "That was from your new book, right? Nice stuff. I'm sorry I didn't get here sooner. I had to leave a dinner that should have been over earlier."

"You didn't need to do that."

"Yes, I did. And I'm glad, too. This was far more enjoyable. I want to talk with you about it sometime, but right now I do have to run."

"I understand. I'm grateful that you came."

On his way, he stopped to speak to Grace and Paul, and they followed him toward the exit, Paul giving me an A-Okay sign without looking my way.

The remaining women, Nada included, circled me, and took turns ensuring that I was occupied with questions: What inspired me to write the book? Why did I choose the female perspective? Did I write every day? Did I read people's manuscripts when asked?

"Do you drink when you write?" Justinia asked, deliberately prodding for a shock to the older women. "I've heard that most famous writers have to drink in order to write."

"I don't drink much. Maybe that's why I'm not famous. I'm too careful."

"Then stop being cautious." Justinia leaned closer, whispered. "I'm on my way to Hagger's. There's a hot band. Want to come?"

"I need to stay here. But I would like to spend time with you."

"I know you would." She clucked her cheek and clicked her red nails together like castanets. She liked adding her personal sounds to an atmosphere.

The reading itself had lasted forty-seven minutes, the reception thirty. It was remarkably true to form.

I had brought no copies of *Fathers*, but Nada announced that the library had a copy. She told me my reading was the best-attended for the year, and I knew she had single-handedly rounded up most of the crew. But she hadn't roped Justinia. The young one had a nice rule or two of her own.

I drank two cups of punch and let Nada press a napkin with two cookies into my hand. I put them in my coat pocket. I thanked them all, sincerely, and went outside.

It was cold and quiet, the quaint streetlamps like tiny frozen moons. I felt good.

"I guess you showed me."

I turned to see Grace. She had come from behind me. "I wasn't trying to show you anything," I said. "It's difficult to save a seat for someone who comes late. Why didn't you hang around? I thought you left with our colleagues."

"I left the building, not you. They went on. I've been sitting in the car. Who is the girl child?"

"Justinia, a friend to one of my students."

"Untidy little creature."

I laughed. It was an apt description. It revealed, too, an edge of jealousy and thus Grace's fondness for me.

"Are you coming to my place?" she said.

Of course I was. And so I told her.

I parked even farther from her house than usual, around the end of the block, near a driveway where no car ever appeared. It was a ridiculous request that I never park in the drive if we were going to bed together. Who would stop by? No one was likely even to stroll up the street or cross the yard. Who would see us? Who would care what we did anyhow? It was a burden she had fashioned for any lover and it was now mine to bear. Arthur come hither, Arthur go yonder. Around the corner. Stay. Walk. Run.

I could have simply gone home, remembered the small accolade of a decent audience and a few colleagues. But there I was, bidden again.

The front door was ajar, and I entered, removed my coat, and laid it over the sofa back. She was in the bedroom already, likely stepping into the shower.

I locked the door, went in the boxy, dull kitchen and lit one of the small candles she kept above the sink. None was new. Perhaps one had been new with me. I lit one, carried it with me, and turned off lamps as I walked to the bedroom. She already had a candle on the dresser.

"You read really well," she said from the bathroom door. She had a toothbrush in one hand, no clothing on at all. It was disarming. Childlike.

"A good audience improves the reading."

"Want to join me in the shower?"

"I do."

We had a pleasant interlude. She was so slight I could lift her as if to carry her away, and hold her beneath the finely spraying shower. We could see each other's faces, feel together the gentle sting, the sluicing of water on our limbs. The spray against the door drummed, sang.

Afterward, sated, she said, "I know how advice irritates you, but maybe the reason *Ghosts* isn't getting published is that you're making the women respond the way you think they would, but you can't know. You're a man, and no matter what they say about human beings being the same, men and women don't see the world the same way."

"So my women characters didn't ring true for you?"

"Not really. Of course, my reaction may not matter. I'm not a writer. But a few passages seemed wrong. Stilted. Like the writer was trying to make the characters say something they wouldn't."

I wasn't angry. Anger is actually foreign to me. I believe she meant well. I traced the hairline of her brow, her cheekbones. I wanted to ask her who she thought she was and why she hurt me. But that's not my way. "Why do you cut your hair so short," I asked, "like a young girl? Aren't you at least fifty?"

She looked stricken. Her whole self withdrew from me.

I wanted to be sorry. I often do.

"Why do you do things like that?" she said. "Why can't you just say you want me to keep my criticism to myself?"

"You have a right to say what you want and do what you want."

"So do you. You don't have to be so goddamned oblique about it." She grabbed a robe, slipped into it, and went into the bedroom.

Shadows in the room moved as they do when you're tired, especially of yourself.

She came back. "Listen, Arthur. Maybe I was too heavy-handed. Your prose is good. I should've said that or nothing at all. You took a chance by reading before a group of strangers, especially a group of women. I could have at least been supportive. I know how sensitive you are." She seemed to expect a response. I didn't know what it was. She took her cigarettes from the nightstand, lit one. The brief, sharp flare made a white mask of her face, accented her eyebrows.

She inhaled, exhaled, looked down at me. "But my mistake doesn't excuse your cruelty."

"Cruelty can be excused sometimes," I said. "But not mine."

It was good enough. She sat down on the bed, put her hand on my chest. "I've been at fault here, too. You're not seeing that girl? The one at the reading?"

"No. I'm not seeing her."

"I couldn't blame you, I guess."

"It would be more than foolish," I said, "especially if it cost me you."

I heard her slight catch of breath.

"I don't want to lose you either," she said, "but you're a real challenge."

"Would you want anything less?"

"No," she said. "Never again."

⟶

I bought Grace a white nightgown. It had long sleeves and a ruffled hem. Pink ribbon was woven into the cuffs and across the bodice. I gauged the length by my own height. I knew exactly where her shoulders came to against me. The saleslady wrapped white tissue paper around it and put it in a white box. She offered to wrap the gift, but I preferred the simplicity.

Grace was astonished. She lifted it out, held it in front of her, then against her. "I had no idea, Arthur, that you thought like this."

"It pleases you, then?"

"It certainly does. I mean, I don't usually wear gowns, as you know. But I *can*." She turned toward her bedroom. "I'll put it on this very minute. I can't imagine. I'm really surprised. I love it. Truly."

I'm not sure she meant exactly that.

"It more than makes up for that book at Christmas."

That sounded more like Grace.

We all judge, but we don't have to *state* the judgment. It's better to swallow some things, even if they choke us. My writing was all I had and I hadn't asked for her opinion.

⌒

Grace's pain troubled me. Pain must be moving. One has to have compassion, or pretend it, assume it, and act from it. What good does it do to see pain and lament it and wish it didn't occur, and then have one more cut of steak, one more dollop of cream?

Grace couldn't have children. She told me that nonchalantly, while looking for a journal she had misplaced. She was a modern literature scholar but rarely mentioned her studies, her specific interests, her findings. I asked her why she and her ex-husband had not had children.

"I couldn't have them," she said, and flipped up a cushion, pulling free the journal that had slipped down by the sofa arm.

"Which may be why the bastard felt free to move on. Biological imperative. See the future. Breed your own caretakers."

She had a new article in the journal, on women's gambling in postwar literature.

"They were doing more than playing cards," she said.

I read it while she watched. It was a jewel piece and I told her so.

"I can write, too," she said, "just not about myself."

I didn't remind her that all writing is about the self. She liked arguments, and sometimes her animated obstinacy wearied me. She was tenacious, too. She should have been through with me long before then.

⟶

Three weeks later, the university went on spring break and my apartment house seemed virtually empty. Occasional sounds indicated a few tenants had remained to study or work. I had no schedule or person to draw me outside myself.

Grace was traveling again, ostensibly alone, but I couldn't know. She had urged me to accompany her and had even offered to pay my way. But this time, my "No" brought an accepting nod.

"You probably wouldn't enjoy it anyway," she said, "and then neither would I."

The last of my manuscripts straggled back, the packages crushed as if the postman had used them for a footstool. In rejection notes, two members of the reading panel had mentioned the point of view: "unbelievable women's voices"; "the ghosts are the real focus here, and they're dull. Might let them speak for themselves. Sorry."

Rain fell Wednesday. My spirits matched the dismal weather.

How, for Pete's sake, could Grace have pinpointed a flaw in my new book when she hadn't even *read* it? She had heard only what I read aloud at the library. How could she know more about my writing than I did?

Actually, in the first version of *Ghosts*, I did have only one speaker, a male one—the ghost himself. But Grace couldn't have known that. Neither could have the rejecting editors. The ghost visited five women's houses. He described the women as they appeared before they knew of his presence, and afterward. As they changed, he changed. He matched their basest imaginings. But he became a character I didn't like, and I couldn't wrap up the book. He disgusted me. Of course I knew that he became disgusting only because of the females' reaction to him, but that didn't matter. I couldn't feel compassion or pity for him. He had to go. I believe in moral fiction, in the writer's responsibility to deplore that which is abhorrent in the human species and to make it abhorrent in his writing. If he fails, he furthers the very attitudes he wants to eradicate. John Gardner. *On Moral Fiction.* Good man, though not a powerful writer. I enjoyed his treatment of Grendel.

In the second version of *Ghosts*, the one Grace and the other critics-at-large had so quickly rejected, the women tell the story. It's a stormy evening—screeching wind, flickering weak candlelight, groaning doors, shadow limbs whipping against windows—and the women have stopped talking about the book-of-the-month and have lapsed into ghost stories. Each tells a personal experience, her encounter with a ghost in her own home. Since the women can describe the ghost only through themselves, he becomes what they are, not what he is. They never realize they're talking about the same man, the same spirit. But the reader should realize it. And so far, not one reader had done so.

I stacked the manuscripts in the closet with the others. You can't make people publish you. You can't turn the whole world around. You can't decide to be the greatest. When you're fifty, you can't be twenty.

I was agitated. Miserable. Forever no good.

I went up to Jack's apartment. It was mid-break, Wednesday night, but perhaps he had come back early. Maybe he would welcome company, would have a cup of coffee or a beer with his teacher. Maybe look pleased at my presence, man to man, artist to artist, something that would redeem my pride a little. I knocked very lightly, unwilling to disturb a young talent. He was home, in all his arrogant glory—shirtless, dark hair spreading wide across his chest, narrowing toward his waist. His hipbones protruded. A lean and hungry young man, at the moment a little angry.

"Yeah?" he said.

"I wondered if you'd be back," I said. "I'm glad to see you are."

"I haven't left. I may take off tomorrow. It depends on the weather. My car's not too reliable."

Behind him, a lithe form rose from the sofa. Sarah. The fine woman. I was glad for Jack. He deserved someone good and unused.

"I thought we might have a drink together, but I see you have company."

He glanced over his shoulder. She was out of view.

"Yeah. Some other time, maybe."

"Certainly. Good night. You have a pleasant break."

When the door closed, I stood for a moment, imagining myself in Jack's room. How would it be to look on other men and women and feel within yourself a resounding belief that you were fine, absolutely fine, worthy of only their best attention? He owned the whole world.

It's embarrassing to be alone when you don't want to be. I went down to the lobby and recreation room. I read the Mason paper—police reports, city council meetings, and families visiting so-and-sos. I felt the cold draft of someone entering the lobby and looked up to see Justinia approaching.

"We've got no heat in my building," she said. "I thought I'd stay at Jack's place."

"He's not alone."

"So he *is* here."

"Yes."

"Who's with him? Sarah?"

"Could be."

She plopped down beside me, all chill and rosiness. "Bummer," she said. "I may go up there anyway."

"You don't really want to cause Jack any unpleasantness, do you?"

"I don't? You got anything else in mind?"

"I could provide you with a comfortable sofa."

"How about warmth? You got any warmth stashed away?" She pronounced it "warm-eth." It was charming because it was unintentional. And she needed to be distracted.

We went upstairs.

She wanted to see a copy of *Fathers*. She stood in my kitchen while I put on the teakettle, propping her left foot against the white doorjamb, and examining my photo on the book jacket. "You were lots younger. When was this?"

"Some years ago. Too many."

"Why haven't you published more? What about the story you read from? Is that in a book yet?"

"It's in a book, just not a published one."

"Pay somebody to publish it."

"You don't understand this field, so best not give advice."

"I read books," she said.

That was a proper stance. She often stumbled onto a pouty righteousness that was winning, if not truly persuasive.

"Yes, you do," I said. "Keep at that."

"I will. You get another one published."

I almost echoed her "I will," but there's something pathetic about claiming what you will do if you haven't been able to do it so far. Besides, she wasn't the type of woman who deserved a better man than I already was.

We easily ended up in bed together because we had already established that extension of our relationship. She liked me and was grateful to me for that brief rescue a short time past. But she loved herself. She loved her body. She stretched it, rolled, posed, purred. She really did purr. She made a low, watery, gurgling sound deep in her throat. Once she put her hand on my scalp, rubbed the skin in a circular motion. It stopped me for a few minutes. Later, when I returned from the bathroom, she said, "You know what I thought? Right in the middle of it? When I was rubbing your head, I thought, why, he's like a basketball, round belly, round head."

"Did you?"

"Yes."

"And you had to tell me that? Why?"

She dropped her gaze. "Sorry."

She had another glass of wine. She wanted to know the writers I had met, any famous people at all. She wanted *names*—you know, to have and use as her own, having not earned a one. She lay on her back and would occasionally raise one or both legs, flex her muscles.

When she slept, I moved to the living room sofa, and there lay awake for hours. Sometimes I disgust myself. I let them make me nothing at all and I don't even protest. I went in the bedroom, sat on the floor against the wall she was facing. Her mouth parted slightly, but it wasn't ugly. It's odd how something in the young animal might be appealing but be totally repulsive in the old.

She woke suddenly, scrambled up, one hand holding the sheet between her heavy breasts.

"What are you watching me for?"

"Because you're the prettiest thing in the place. I could look at you for hours."

"Well, don't do that when I'm sleeping. It's creepy."

"All right, I won't. You frighten me a little, too." I stood up. "Would you mind going on down to the lobby now? For your sake, I'd rather no one saw you emerge from my room."

Rumpled and tawny, puffy-lipped, she struggled into her clothing and straggled out my door, dragging her coat along the hallway.

I couldn't *think* something into happening, not anger, not love. I could think myself inside out without altering one second of reality. What came, came. Faulkner understood that. All of history recurred each moment and one was caught in it again and again.

I changed the bedding and lay down. I could feel the cold dawn seep under the sills and creep along the floor. I rather welcomed it.

CHAPTER 20

MASON, SPRING BREAK, 1992

It rained again, most of the day, and then the temperature began to drop. An ice storm was on its way.

I slept off and on, waking in the night just enough to know it wasn't time and going under again. When I finally emerged, ridges of ice blurred the periphery of the windows and I could have been anywhere.

The muted light fell on my manuscript. I remembered crisp air around a small house, remembered looking through windows into hazy rooms, remembered rows of blue notebooks in a bookcase. Nada's house. Nada's books.

Nada herself. I could see her perfectly—it was a dear face and I didn't know why it had appeared. The usual calm had settled on me, the assurance of methodical steps presenting themselves appropriately, but I was at the same time perplexed and reluctant. One can long to resist. No, that is not quite accurate. One can wish to yearn, and to yearn for something good.

I fixed breakfast as usual, oatmeal and toast, and I sat at the table while the food grew cool. I couldn't eat. I think that was a sign of my fondness and concern for Nada. A new pattern was emerging, which I now recognize: Nada was from my *present* time. She was not a memory or a chance encounter. She was not unkind. She was herself a victim. She was absolutely random, but in the wrong time. I was perplexed, but there the day was, and I was in it.

Whatever steps came next, I took, which is how these things must happen. What I do or don't want has no bearing on events.

Outside, it was so ungodly cold that the air seemed fragile, brittle, like the world might crack if I took one wrong move.

Through town, I drove very slowly to avoid mishaps, but increased speed once I was on the flat, paved road stretching east. It was elevated from the fields and thus visible for some distance, like an invitation. I knew the entire route by heart, probably from my Christmas trip. We remember things we don't notice at the time. A house to the south, perhaps a mile, with smoke rising from the chimney. A silo and barn, likely another house just out of sight. I passed a place where the sharp escarpment ended at a fence, beyond which a frozen pond lay like a silver plate, the cold dawn reflecting smaller rising circles.

About a mile from the dirt road leading to Nada's house, I pulled over to the right, slowly, as much off the pavement as possible, stopped the car and turned off the motor. I stayed inside for a few moments. I thought perhaps I was going to turn around. That was possible. I heard my breath and saw it, little puffs of being alive. Then I got out of the car and began walking. It took care and patience, but it was pleasant enough. I liked the precision of an ice day. Sharp and clean. Perfect.

I trudged to her door, heard the crunch of my passage, my occasional gasps as I nearly fell. The cold seared my throat.

When Nada answered the knock, she didn't look like the same woman, and may not have been. She looked ill, the flesh beneath her eyes swollen and too white, with dark creases under the puff. She hadn't curled her hair. It was thin and straggly straight, an old woman's hair.

"What are you doing out here?" she said.

I had thought she'd open the door immediately, bustle me in with protests about the weather. I was surprised.

"My car slid off the road."

She looked past me to the yard, then beyond, still not opening the door.

"Where?"

"Back toward town. Could I come in, Nada? It's pretty cold out here."

"I'm not ready for company."

I was momentarily stymied—who could have anticipated that response? "Then could I just borrow *your* car? Maybe I could get one of your neighbors to pull me out. Or I could drive to a station."

"What if something happened to mine? What if I needed it before you came back?"

She was having her conversation while I became increasingly chilled and the return to my own vehicle became simultaneously more necessary and more difficult. Still, I acquiesced. That's what one does. I bowed my head to her wishes, and said, "I'm sorry I disturbed you. I can see that you're ill." I turned to leave. I *intended* to leave. But something had happened in her bright mind. Maybe she weighed her former investment against this possible rejection and decided to rein me in. More likely, her insatiable curiosity prompted her change of heart. She wanted to know what I was about.

And she was lonely. That's the impetus for much human behavior. She called after me. "Dr. Blume!"

In seconds, I was inside.

She hadn't yet relinquished control of herself. She stood in the middle of a braided carpet in the overcrowded room, a grainy light falling over her sparse curls and pasty face. "Why didn't you just call me," she said. "Our road is really a bad one."

"The phone lines to my apartment building are out. No one could call. I went out just to find a phone and decided I would drive on out here. Dr. Burch said you often spend the nights in town during bad weather. I was going to take you in."

"What if I'd already been in town? You might have been stuck out here for nothing. Isn't that right?"

"Yes, it is right. I was foolish to come. If you'll let me use your phone, I'll get out of your hair as quickly as possible."

"It's over there," she said, nodding at a small table next to a deep, wide chair.

A wall furnace kicked on, blew a stream of warm air toward us. The room was already stifling. Small porcelain dolls were everywhere, deathly white with vivid, painted clothing. Doilies everywhere, myriad sizes and colors. Past times brought front and future. She filled every minute with a sign of herself. Produce, produce, produce. She wore a pink corduroy robe with a wide lapel. Peppermint. She reminded me of an ice cream cone. She tightened the sash.

I pretended to call a service station, though the number was actually for time and temperature. She listened avidly, I know, because the kitchen was a blank section of the house until I hung up the phone and joined her. Then it was a flurry of activity. She scurried to heat coffee, warm lemon cake, set two places at the kitchen table, fold napkins, prattle about the state of the house and of herself and explain how she wasn't prepared, but did enjoy company.

Cold sun poured across the room.

I watched this happen. The same is probably true of her. We were both interested in the unfolding.

I explained my other concern about my responsibilities to her. "I want to apologize," I said. "I know I've been hard on you in class, and that I've resisted praising your writing. I think I have a hangup about women writers." This caused raised brows and a snapped nod. She might have been thinking *You know it, mister,* but she wisely held her tongue. "I know I shouldn't have that attitude," I continued. "It's old-fashioned and unrealistic and unkind, too. But I find it easier to relate to male students and to their work. I've had trouble, in the past, when I praised a woman's work. Some of them have. . . ."

She completed the sentence. "Caused trouble."

"A little. Nothing serious. I'm human. If I praise them too much, they think I'm their springboard to success. They think I'll get them an agent, a publisher."

I could see her clicking away this new admission, testing it, fitting it into her own mental slots. "Is that why you came to Mason? You had trouble?"

"I wasn't talking about trouble. I was describing a general attitude."

My willingness to admit weakness emboldened her. "Then why did you come to Mason? Everyone wants to know."

"You mean Dr. Burch wants to know? Because I can teach creative writing here, and it's a tenure-line position. But I've been botching my job. You're a good writer, and I haven't acknowledged that or pushed you in the right directions. I'm sorry."

"You have been rude to me," she asserted, one finger tapping that flaw into the table. "Just in class. The students tell me you don't like my kind of writing and that I shouldn't take what you say seriously."

"They're right," I said, and won the old girl completely. Her lips parted, her eyes brightened, rounder, plum. But she still took nearly an hour to get moving. I praised her poems, recited more lines, questioned her gently about her fiction, and told her I would very much like to read it when she felt like sharing it. I phoned the false station again.

"Well, I can't wait indefinitely," I said into the receiver, "because I'm inconveniencing a colleague who doesn't feel too well."

Nada was pleased. She had become my equal.

I hung up the phone, raised both hands in exasperation, and said, "They won't say when they're coming. I'm going to walk on down to my car. I've put you out long enough."

"You don't have to go."

"I'm getting frustrated waiting, especially since you're not feeling well and can't be at ease with someone in the house. I came out here to make you feel better, not discomfit you. I'll be fine."

She let me don my coat and gloves. She trailed me to the door with one more, "You can just wait here. I don't mind." But I insisted. I opened the door. I bowed—indicating a gratitude I genuinely felt. "It's a piercing cold, isn't it?" I walked gingerly across the slick porch and down the steps. "Call me if you need anything," I said, without looking back. "And let me read more of your work when you're ready."

Her words touched me on the shoulder.

"You get in here," she said. "You're being foolish."

So I returned.

Twice she could have seen my back.

She fluttered herself ready to drive into town. She had to dress, to straighten up the kitchen.

"I never leave a mess. I leave the house the way I want to find it when I come home. That way I get a lift just closing the door behind me. It'll be nice having company on the way in. I wouldn't have gone because of the ice. This way, I get company, and a ride in, and I do have friends I can stay with. I often do that, you know, stay with friends? This is a little adventure, isn't it? You and I taking a dangerous drive together." That thought brought her still, to lock eyes with me. "What happens if we go off the road in my car? I can't walk far, and not in cold at all. It saps the heart. All the blood has to be warmed."

I reassured her. "I'll take care of you. We won't have an accident. I will be so cautious that you could even fall asleep. I'll also repay you with a nice dinner, even a movie. How's that? The roads will be clear in town, at least by evening."

"You don't need to repay me. You were checking on me, right? You were out here for me?"

A sincere question made her voice somewhat querulous, and I saw the sharp scrutiny distinguished in that pale blue gaze. She was nobody's fool, had never been. She was right to be suspicious.

"I was checking on you, yes. But if you're uneasy with me, don't come along. Be easy on yourself. I can get the station again, have them come on out."

"Why would I be uneasy with you?" she said, as if I might inadvertently give her a reason she already knew.

"Women have their reasons," I said, "and have to trust them. What else can they do?"

"We do," she said. "Women have to be careful."

I sat on the wide arm of a spacious plush chair. I could see hints of the other rooms, a frosty window on the north side. I had once looked in that window particularly.

"You're welcome to stay at my place, if you think it's proper."

"Oh, you!" with a feisty, flirting wave of a seventy-three-year-old hand.

She washed and dried the plates and utensils we had used. She put them away. She was eliminating any trace of my visit. She may have also been waiting to be at peace with the direction the day had taken.

"How much fiction have you written?" I asked.

"Lots of it. Maybe more than poems. It's easier, isn't it? You can write up to something or around it, and then go on to explain it. A poem is just there, all naked."

"That's well said."

She dried her hands on a yellow terrycloth towel. She took a small tube from the window sill, squeezed lotion into her palms, then vigorously rubbed it into her hands.

"It's vanilla," she said. "Isn't it nice?"

I assumed it was. "Yes."

"You want to see how much fiction I've written?" she said. "I'll bet it surprises you. Come on, let me show you."

She led me into the nearby study, stopped before the shelves I knew were there, and gestured toward them with open hand. "See."

"All of these?"

"Most of them. From here," she ran her finger across almost two shelves of notebooks, "to here. Fiction. I have others, too. And I may write that many more before I'm through."

"That's really impressive. I mean it."

"I would let you read them."

"Would you?"

She didn't know, surely, how many, many times a writer hears "I would let you read," as though the imposed burden is a gift, as though his own writing time has no value, as though he would of course rather immerse himself in someone else's creation, even if it stank.

"Yes, I would," she said, "and I don't let just anybody see my stories. Do you want to?"

"Yes, I do. Very much."

"Is it because the students think I'm a good writer?"

"Because I know you are," I said.

That was a good thing to say. She had longed to hear that. We decided that I should take all the volumes at one time and read them over the days remaining in spring break. She packed them up for me. In pillowcases. I would never have thought of that. It was a simple, practical, homey solution.

I wasn't actually thinking of her manuscripts at all. They were just part of the package.

She gave me her keys. A university office key was on her keychain. I put the books in the trunk, started the car to warm. I scraped ice from the windshield The cold hurt my eyes, stiffened my skin. It was all perfect. I walked back to the house. The sun glistened on the ice, fine and piercing, blind-white. I lifted a hand-sized stone from those edging her flowerbeds and put it in my pocket. It was another simple thing to do. She bundled out, locked the door. I helped her from the porch, guided her carefully to the car, assisted her inside.

The gravel ruts were easy to navigate, but at the slight rise to the main road I sped up to avoid sliding. "Hold on," I said.

"Oh," she said, the sound lasting until the car was over the hump and pointing toward town.

"I'm sorry," I said. "I had to do that, but we're all right now." Warm air from the heater rose, touched my face, but I could feel, too, the chill from the door window. "It's a straight shot the rest of the way."

She was interested in something ahead of us, to the left, and leaned forward, craning as if trying to get a clear picture. I knew what she saw. The dark object was quite recognizable at that distance. My car. Where it was not supposed to be. Fully visible. I thought I might stop there. I would say, *Look! Someone's pulled me out. What a break!*

"What should we have for dinner?" I asked her. "Do you like Italian?"

"Why didn't you call the gas station and tell them not to come?"

See how bright she was in her own way? She wanted me to know that my lapse had not gone without notice.

"We can stop by the station when we reach town. We'll probably get there before they leave, anyhow, or meet them on the way. We'll wave them down. I don't want to cause an unnecessary trip for anyone in weather like this."

Her hope was palpable. She was willing the truth not to be.

We were approaching my vehicle. She looked at it as we passed, her head turning as if by continuing to stay focused on it, she might return to the time before it. She raised her gaze upward.

"Wasn't that your car?"

I didn't respond. We both knew the answer.

"It wasn't off the road," she said.

We were nearing the steepest part of the escarpment. The sun glazed over the road before us, over the windshield slush. I accelerated. We might fly past the moment, completely past it.

She gripped the door handle.

"I want to go home, Dr. Blume," she said.

"I'm very fond of you. Genuinely fond. Do you know that?"

"Yes," she blurted, "yes, I do. But I would like to go home, please."

My arm jerked to the left and, so smoothly, we slid sideways to the top edge of the slope, bumped over, bounced. She shrieked, grabbed the dash, shrieked again. We could have turned over. We teetered, slid a few feet more and stopped before a wire fence.

"Here we are," I said. I reached for my door handle.

"What are you doing? Why did you crash us?"

"You have to get out." I balanced myself against the car to edge around it, and still my footing was precarious. I opened her car door. She had one hand on the dash, one at the base of her throat. I leaned in, grasped both her wrists and tugged. She squealed "What! what!" and tried to jerk free. I braced myself against the inside of the open door, one foot on the floorboard edge, and yanked hard, harder, down and out. She fought me, wriggled and rolled. She was heavy and old, and she panted jagged, uneven gasps. I twisted her out of the car, down, onto the ice, back. The thick coat bound her. We both slipped and she spun a half-circle on the ice like an odd-shaped top. I fumbled the stone from my pocket only to drop it. It skittered away. But I didn't need it after all. I grabbed a frozen branch from the ground and though she tried to scramble to her knees and away from me, she remained in a seated position and thus made the blow easier. She had helped me all along without knowing it. See? I swung the branch at the back of that round head and she bent forward from the blow. She struggled her torso erect, sat stunned and weaving. I stepped in front of her and her plum eyes opened wide. Her mouth was agape. "I'm sorry," I said, and I truly was. Two things can be true at once. She tried to scoot backward. I moved behind her and swung the branch again, harder, but aiming to strike her with the same portion of the branch. I fell to my knees. I grabbed her left shoulder and pulled her backward, laying the branch behind her, so her head would rest just there, just there. Her mouth was closed now, the edges of her lips drooping, an upside-down smile. Her face seemed younger.

I bent to determine if she breathed. I could see a tiny, hunched, black shadow in her pupils. Me.

Then came the walk back to my car, the return to Nada's, and the transfer of the pillowcases to my trunk. I took Nada's purse from the car, slipped the keychain inside, and carried the bag over to her. Such stillness. Peace. She had been good to me in her way. I opened her purse, removed the university key from the chain. Margaret didn't deserve any triumph over Nada.

The ice hadn't even begun to melt. I wouldn't leave a trace at all.

I've seen documentaries where prey is brought down, not dead, lying on its side, head up, while the predators begin their meal. It is sickening, but reassuring, implying there is within a body the ability to rescue itself from the most horrifying situation. There is a poem about that ability, about screams becoming song in the victim's ear. It is a small tribute to human strength.

◆

When you step into a cosmic order, you know it. You act without worry. Every molecule of your body hums perfection. That's how I was on the drive back from Nada's. I wasn't unfeeling. I grieved for her in my way. But you can grieve and not show a sign; you can grieve and feel the world is harmonious, too. I don't know why people have to have one extreme or the other, light and dark, good and evil. I hadn't grieved for the others, that's true. I was only the instrument of their undoing. Faulkner's Mink Snopes, in *The Hamlet*, undid Houston. Mink had paid the penalty imposed upon him, had twisted his nature to do so, and had fixed on the day he could say *There, done and done.* He had earned his moment of glory and justice. Houston took it from him. Then Mink took it from Houston. Mink recreated the future that was already past to him. No one should mess around with the peace we've made for ourselves.

So I did grieve. I think I did. How am I supposed to know for sure? I could bring to mind my final view of Nada, all toad-splayed on the hard ground. Pink and lily white. Virgin Mary. Ice.

◆

I like the half-second of life in eyes. I just thought of that, and I'm trying to be honest here. I said I'd tell everything and that's one thing I have to tell. There's more passion in that half-second than in some whole lives. Some people might prefer living it over and over.

◆

I went to the campus first, because I had Nada's key. The parking lots and walkways were solid sheets of ice. I skidded along, a dedicated professor who had to get to the office, weather be damned.

The key was a master key. It opened not only the main door, but the department office. I assumed it would open all the doors. I went to Nada's little slice of office. I was looking for whatever she had found to be important. I had earned the right.

Inside Nada's filing cabinet I found folders labeled by class titles, about twelve of them. I flipped quickly through a few files and my admiration grew. The labels were miscues. *We* were in there. The faculty. Grace's file included copies of Grace's vita, old and new, department evaluations, grade records, a list of former addresses, a copy of a letter to a Florida courthouse requesting a copy of "her" divorce decree (the return address was Nada's), the requested decree, a Florida newspaper article announcing the marriage of Dr. Walter E. Burch to Deborah Mae Chesterfield, crumpled personal notes to Grace from "Leonard" (none other than Dr. Walsh), a stained and crumpled list of prescriptions. And—a list of men's names, in Nada's handwriting, with every loop filled black. My name was there. So were two other colleague's names. Not Harper's. Not Loeffle's. I left the list in the file.

Nada Petrovich, trash-can historian, excavating the debris of the civilization resting upon her.

She hadn't locked the cabinet. Was that contempt? Hope? Did she know that the prying would undo the one who pried as much, if not more than, herself? Maybe she liked the possibility of discovery. She wasn't a coward.

My folder was deceptively thick. It held a complete photocopy of *Fathers* and its reviews, copies of my vita, letters of reference, and two hand-written lists. One was a record of my in-class comments about *her* work, apparently quoted verbatim. She had noted the date and the names of classmates who, I guess, could serve as witnesses. Witnesses to what? My limited praise of her efforts? My lack of praise? Misunderstanding? Was she planning a grievance complaint? The other list was of cities where I had worked, along with the inclusive dates. It intrigued me only a little, because the information was readily available in my vita. But then I saw a similar yellow sheet edging the tab of another file—Harper's. There, too, a record of cities and dates, a few with a name penciled nearby. I removed both lists. His file was quite full, orderly, some papers stapled together, some clipped. I took everything but his vita, transcripts, and old student rosters. I looked in Loeffle's file, too. A note of thanks to Nada, a birthday card, a photo of his daughter, and a copy of three local newspaper police reports with Loeffle's speeding violations highlighted in yellow.

When I left her office and looked back, the winter sun was slanting across the flowers on her file cabinet. It was a lovely scene.

Before reaching the department exit, I passed Harper's office and wondered if he were in there. It was possible. Anything was possible. I knocked lightly. "Harper?" I inserted the master key, unlocked and opened the door, and stepped inside. The closeness nearly sucked the breath from me. The limited floor space was filled with uneven stacks of newspapers, magazines, journals, catalogues, used library books, new books. A sole straight-backed chair sat before the desk, certainly not offering students any reason to linger. The rolling, padded chair behind the desk was lopsided, black-and-white checked, from some other office, other décor. A ginger jar, blue and white, rested precariously on a stack of graded papers on the desk. I glanced at the paper beneath it. It had been graded. "F—No thought, no effort, no pass." I had heard that he let students look at their grades, but he kept their papers.

I stood perfectly still, scanned the room, closed my eyes as he so often did. Could this be a lair? It had the stench of disuse and lethargy, even decay. Could we in any conceivable way, however minuscule, be alike? I didn't want that to be true, but how to know? Dissecting one's own subterranean self is challenge enough.

I left then. What had to be done had been done.

⌐

A lungfish stays in its pond while the water dries up above it, around it, and the fish stops being fish, is mud-caked semideath, waiting on water and life. I wonder if it has a sense of self and of time, and knows when the drying has reached its own flesh and it will breathe no more. Is there a gasp? Does it inhale mud through gills and swallow mud through gaping mouth?

A locust waits seventeen years for one destructive path. A wide swath, worthy of the wait.

I'm a patient man, but by practice, not nature.

⌐

I went to the twenty-four-hour Megamart. A customer was paying for orange juice and potato chips. I coughed. "Sorry," I said. I bought tea, lemon juice, clover honey, cough syrup, cold tablets. At the register, I coughed again.

"This weather can get you down," the clerk said.

"It sure can. I had a devil of a time getting here, but I need something."

She was tall, heavy-torsoed, and round-shouldered, but friendly enough. "They're getting the streets clear now," she said. "It's supposed to start warming later, or tomorrow for sure."

"They're not clearing the campus, though. I tried to get to my office."

She didn't respond, but she had noticed me enough, and I knew she had heard. We all hear far more than we acknowledge.

"You have a good day," she said when I left.

I drove home cautiously. The city road crew had already salted two of the roads. The parking lot was dotted with a few cars, all ice-covered. The sun encased the whole apartment building in a halo of white. I walked slowly up the stairs. It didn't matter at all who saw or heard me, because my purpose for being out and about was evident. I was sick. And I had tried to go to the office in spite of my condition. Had wasted considerable time. I was an ill and frustrated man.

I went into my own place, turned the fire on under the teakettle, and put on light music. I recall it seemed a glorious moment, stopped into itself, inviolable, forever whole. Not mine. The reverse.

The rest of the day and into early evening I established my cold. I poured some of the cough syrup down the sink, followed by three of the cold tablets. I drank tea. Occasionally I coughed. It's better to live what you must pretend.

I had to wait for dark to retrieve the pillowcases of notebooks. So, I did other work. I went through the papers I had taken from Harper's folder. She had copied all travel records from his department file. Of course, he had asked for reimbursement only for trips to conferences, so not *all* his trips were noted. They were jotted in a column on yellow legal paper, and across from them, here and there, the name of a city, of a young woman, and the date of her disappearance, or the date when a body was found, a nameless woman, again young. With a dark line she had highlighted a few correspondences.

That explained her list of my employment dates. She had begun to chart me, too. Wily, wily woman. Mistress of traps.

Nada had copied postcards that Paul had sent to various department members, each with his one-sentence style of discourse: "Glad to be gone and sorry you had to stay." "Wonderful fresh air here, untainted by fast food on every corner." "If they'll let me live in the university library, I will not return." The postmark cities and dates were on the list, but with a blank space beside them. That must have caused her disappointment—to have his exact location and nothing foul to associate it with. Did she really think she had a murderer? Would she have let him walk the halls, buy her chocolate? Maybe. They aspire to the thrill of danger from a safe position. She wasn't a young woman, not likely to be victim. She was going to capture him or make him up. What was the difference to her?

But she had taken too big a leap from the evidence, conjectured too far for accuracy. Here's what she had: a newspaper photo with an accompanying short paragraph about the recent high school graduate (from a small southeastern town) who had enlisted and planned to travel the world with the army. The young Paul Harper was shrunken inside the uniform, his broad shoulders suggesting a skeleton beneath the cloth, his smile either timid or sardonic, depending on one's encounter with the boy; a skewed, faint, but legible copy of the dishonorable discharge of Paul Isaac Harper, the date eight months after the newspaper article.

And the true find: notes and letters concerning a female student's claim that Dr. Paul Harper had plagued her with obscene phone calls. The dates placed the charge during his first years in Mason. She had recognized his voice. She had hung up on him each time. She didn't want to drop the class so late, but she wasn't going back. The college letter was a careful, sparse record. No formal charges, Dr. Harper. They realized that the student might be attempting to avoid a failing grade. But another similar charge could result in his not receiving tenure. Even after tenure, such an incident would be grounds for dismissal with cause.

Dishonorable discharge. He had lied to my face. I didn't really mind. Lies are a basic protection of any weak or captive *speaking* creature. Even subservience can be a lie.

Obscene phone calls. Perhaps he could *aspire* to murder, but he was no man. He didn't risk himself. He couldn't even show his face to his victims.

Nada couldn't put him together because he had no substance. He was a weakness looking for form. He was a piece of filth floating loose in the dark.

When night fell, I slept for a few hours. Then, after midnight, I arose, filled two pillowcases with towels and sheets, and carried them downstairs. I stepped out into a clear, sharp-star night. Space, space, space, and me underneath it all. The store clerk had been right. The night wasn't quite as cold; a thaw was coming. I exchanged the pillowcases. I was unlikely to encounter anyone, especially anyone who would notice the pillowcases held something other than laundry. I met no one.

Upstairs, I spread newspaper over the table, put on my gloves, and stacked the notebooks and a box of file folders on the dining table. Nada's whorls and scribbles decorated a few of the covers, and each was identified with a Roman numeral on the spine, "Volume I," etc., followed by inclusive dates. She was orderly. I labeled my own folders as I would a working draft—"WD chp. 1," "WD chp. 2," and so on. After all, naming something is the first step in owning it.

There remained the problem of the empty binders. I couldn't burn them. I didn't have a fireplace, and besides, the metal rings wouldn't burn. With a butcher knife and scissors I cut and ripped them apart. It was very difficult work, especially as I wasn't feeling well. And—Paul Harper should be grateful—I cut up the contents of his file along with mine. I put the pieces and shreds in the pillowcases. Then I went outside again, to drive behind dormitories and distribute all that remained into trash bins.

At my apartment building, I carried up the pillowcases of linen. Jack Goff was coming down the stairway from my floor.

"Did you get away at all?" I asked.

"Nope." He was in sock feet, dressed in rumpled blue slacks and blue collarless sweater. He looked tired, even gaunt. "I got sick," he said. "I couldn't go anywhere. I'm just up now to get a Coke or something."

There it was, a clue of the pattern. I make up a cold that he already has.

"Me, too," I said. "I bought some cough syrup and cold tablets if you need them."

"No. I just want a Coke."

"Hot tea would be better. With lemon and honey."

He was already taking the steps down, and stood just below me. Our eyes were at the same level.

"No," he said. "No thanks."

At that precise moment, a scrap of blue canvas, a tiny little jagged scrap no larger than my thumbnail, fluttered from my coat sleeve to the floor. I watched it float down.

"See you," he said, and descended the stairs. I picked up the scrap.

In my rooms, I flushed that piece, and searched every bit of the coat and my clothing for others. I found none. I felt chilled—"to the bone," as my mother often said. Then I truly did have a cough.

Saturday, I slept. The entire day. Long and deep.

CHAPTER 21

Three years after my mother's surgery, I returned home to spend the summer. I know that seems odd, since I wasn't exactly happy around her, but I wasn't very happy anywhere else, either. Sometimes people or problems get embedded in your head and you worry them like a dog with a bone. You feel that just one more visit, one more look, one more word, and you'll understand something that will enable you to slough off the bad feeling and get on with your life. I imagine that's why people stalk one another, bombard others with letters or phone calls, bash in windows, doors, heads. They want to understand. They need closure. They can't believe that the slight sour taste is all there is. Like the crazy monkey mother from the special I watched long ago, they think this baby will nurse if it's just shaken around a bit.

When I turned onto her road, I stopped the car. Something was wrong. I knew I had made the right turn, yet this wasn't the road I had known all my life. It was level, and asphalt instead of dirt, a smooth black curving line all the way to the yard. And the house, too, was different. It was clean, newly white, with light blue shutters. They had been black or gray before—some non-color. A white station wagon was in the driveway. Company? At my mother's?

Once cued to the changes, I noticed more improvements: An abandoned tractor wheel had been hauled away; a cord of wood was piled at the fence line; the fence wire stretched tight and unbroken, no busted or leaning poles; trees fronting the house had been trimmed, the raw patches painted white.

I expected to find my mother just back from a ride to town, and to encounter the driver preparing to leave. But there was no company in the house. She had seen me coming and was standing in the living room when I opened the front door.

"I'm surprised to see you," she said. She wore a blue housedress with a wide belt. She had gained much weight, mostly in the torso. Her abdomen thrust forward like a plump hen, an image so common to older women. Her hair was clasped at the nape of her neck. I didn't know her. She may have been my mother, but something had shifted.

"I'm surprised, too," I said.

The living room furniture was all new: not even the kind of furniture that had surrounded me all my life. It was modern, light cream, with plush chocolate and yellow pillows everywhere. The round end tables were also revolving bookracks. The wide easy chairs had been replaced with two recliners, a contour lamp behind each. She could twist the light wherever she needed it. It was an airy reading room, completely foreign to me.

"I feel like I'm in the wrong house."

"I decided to do the place up."

"Have you redone everything?"

"Just down here. I keep the upstairs shut off. I got a washer and dryer, too."

She had turned toward the kitchen. I followed her.

"I thought about getting a new range, but I don't want to get used to a new stove." She was filling the kettle. "You had lunch yet?"

"Yes. You've tiled the kitchen. What else?"

"This is linoleum. It just looks like tile. I got a freezer in the basement."

"Whose car's in the driveway?"

"Mine."

She knew. She knew how I felt. She glanced at me quickly, kind of slyly, and went on making her tea. "Belle taught me how to drive," she said.

There was a time when those looks of hers, those from-the-side glimpses, were beautiful to watch. The profile, the slanted, dusky lids, the dark-iris sliver like a hiding moon. But now even her eyes had gone. A slight fold of skin at the outer edges made the eyes seem shorter, rounder. No sloe-eyed deer here. Wily.

"Belle said I learned real fast. I could've been driving all this time."

"I would've taught you long ago."

"I wasn't ready to learn. You have to get ready to know things."

"Where'd you get the money? Did you sell some land?"

She didn't answer.

"I asked where the money came from."

"It was my money, Arthur. Watch your voice with me."

"You never had money when I needed it."

She was agitated. When she brought her tea to the table, her hand shook. When she tried to lift it, tea splattered over the edge onto the saucer and table. She wiped up the spill. Holding the cup with both hands, she managed a few sips. I got a larger cup from the cabinet, emptied part of her tea into it. Now she'd have to deliberately dump it to make a mess.

She drank a little. "Common sense," she said. "I should've thought of that. A bigger cup's all I needed." Then, with that second-thought glance at me, "But I liked that little cup. That's why I took it."

For a while, she didn't read. She asked me about my job. I could hear the effort to keep her voice slow. Her fingers traced the arm of the chair. Her foot swung. At the hollow of her throat, a vessel pulsed strongly and rapidly. Though she didn't really sway, the strain of not swaying wearied us both. All she had to do was let go. It was going to happen. I'd come home at the wrong time.

She read from four or five books that afternoon—flip a few pages, skim, skim, flip, pick up another. Drank tea, tea, tea.

She insisted on fixing supper. She ate more than I'd ever seen her eat. Just before the fork touched her lips, her tongue appeared, slipped under the fork, guided it in. A loving eater. The style of a fat woman. I've seen it a thousand times, that little give-away of pleasure.

I lay awake that night in my upstairs room. It was hot, miserably so, the air heavy and moist, unmoving, old. I heard her in the kitchen, opening the refrigerator. Heard water running in the pipes. Once I thought she came to the bottom of the stairs and I was sickened at the very possibility of her coming to *my* room. If she had, I don't know what I'd have done. Suffered.

I knew she was ill. I couldn't care, because of the car and because of money. I think I wanted her to go off the deep end so I could rummage around, maybe find some records, maybe get her into a hospital and have the right to investigate her accounts. These weren't loving, admirable traits. But they were human. I had always taken care of her, taken care of myself, but without knowing anything, without the *wherewithal.* She swallowed up help, and lasted and lasted.

The next morning, in the midst of cleaning up the breakfast dishes, she clutched her arms above the elbows and bowed her head. Her hands were still sudsy and white foam dripped on her dress.

"What's the matter?"

She didn't answer.

"What's the matter? Are you ill?"

"Just leave me alone." Her face had blanched. Her eyes were stricken and wild. She suddenly dropped her arms, crossed the kitchen, and went out the back door. She paced in the yard. I went out on the back porch.

"Don't watch me," she said.

"I want to help."

"Go away."

I went as far as the steps, watched her from there. She darted one look at me and walked out of sight around the side of the house. I went inside, followed her passage by the windows. This was different, this new madness—she seemed almost able to control it. She walked as far as the downdip of the road, then stopped. She put her hands on her hips. In a few moments, she turned around and came back slowly. She came in the front door and I was waiting on her.

"What is it?"

"You can't let anything alone, can you?"

I followed her into the kitchen again.

"I get these scared spells every now and then," she said. "I have to run them off. That's what the doctor said to do, so that's what I do."

"Hormones?"

"Something like that."

"Afraid of what?"

"Nothing. Everything. I just feel afraid for a while. That's all. Nothing you can do about it."

I didn't actually want to do anything about it. I wanted to see it happen again. I wanted it to happen again and again, so much, so strong, so long and ugly, that it ran itself out of being.

I stayed for a month of my summer writing time. Belle Wilson wanted to know how I liked all the changes. She checked the house out as if it were still new to her and might even *be* hers someday. She reminded me of a starling, the squat, ragged-tailed, squabbling bird. They fill any atmosphere with quarrels and filth. They swarm. And though she was alone, she left the sense of having swarmed and laid claim. Her name was a grand disguise.

"I told your mother that money wouldn't do her any good when she was dead and gone. The interest alone could spruce this place up as long as she lives."

She had black-cap hair, slat-hips, pebble eyes. Another ugly woman.

Some are pretty, some are ugly. You have to read all the signs to know one's true nature.

Before I left Georgia, I went to visit Mr. Watson. He said Belle Wilson was a good woman. She was on all the town committees— beautification, day care for working mothers, library, food pantry, free clinic. "She wouldn't be out to take your mother for anything. Belle's a helper." He said the whole town had always known my mother had money. Her parents had had plenty, and then there was insurance, too, and maybe even some from a lawsuit.

"Didn't you wonder," I asked, "why I bought that old junker car? Why I waited to go to school? Why I worked all those years?"

"I thought it was the way you did things, Arthur. You mulled 'em over first. You went slow. I did talk to your mother about you, though, right after you came to work for me. I told her I thought you needed help of some kind."

"What'd she say?"

"She said you were just like her, and she was helping you all she could."

"And that sounded right to you?"

"Kind of. I tried talking to you, too. Remember? I asked what you wanted to do for yourself. You said, 'Be left alone.'"

I remembered that. I remember he said, "Okay, Arthur," and walked back to the stockroom. He had taken it as so wholly and easily true. I hadn't meant it. I hadn't meant for him to leave me alone every way under the sun. Kids think adults can read intent and desire from thin air in spite of all negation.

"I would've helped you more," he said, "if I'd known how."

It's not the money, you understand. It's the value implied. This for that. My hours for a pittance, with salvation behind lock and key. She let me labor. She stayed mute and mad and let me struggle for just a fingerhold. I know she was ill. I forgive her for it.

⟶

The chemicals in the brain get in a pattern sometimes. Instead of having fear cause a little synapse here and there, the trained brain fires FEAR NOW and the body surges to run and fight and kill and die and there's no place to go and nothing to do so it buzzes crazy, crazy, crazy through every fiber of your being and you jerk-walk like an automaton with slipped gears but in superdrive. That's one slight chemical imbalance. It may or may not occur more than once a day. It can be controlled if the person is intelligent enough to learn how to ride it out so the chemical lessens and the pattern shifts. A person can suffer from more than one imbalance and have to learn many, many controls.

Extreme fear is like peace, because there's no place further to go, no higher terrain, so the senses check out of the body. It's a survival in the moment of death, a rescue of self.

＜—

Maybe there were twelve women. I wouldn't lie about it if I knew for sure.

A person can stumble upon an act so demanded, so necessary, as if it were fueled by rage but without the rage. Maybe even the rage has been stolen. Such acts would be accidents of fate, completed by someone without will.

CHAPTER 22

Sunday morning, I took a cup of coffee downstairs, to the common room, and watched the news. The local stations were still enamored of the disappearing ice storm. Regional people usually like regional wonders, and bad weather can reach legendary status in a matter of hours. Every state I've been in has believed its own weather to be unique. The Mason channel ran pictures of ice on cars, windows, trees, mailboxes; melting icicles against a rising sun.

No mention of Nada.

The local paper didn't print over the weekend and there wasn't much chance Nada would appear in the *Kansas City Star* if she weren't on the local news.

That meant she was still where I had left her, arms open, and no one acknowledging the gesture.

I went back upstairs to my own place. I had furnished it for beauty and comfort: a burgundy sofa with curved wooden legs; a dark blue chair with high back and wide wings; a rose silk chair, threaded with blue, thick-cushioned and armless; a rocker footstool; aged, dark-oak tables; a tall rosewood occasional table, holding a paradise lamp; a framed tapestry, wide but shallow, almost a monochrome of pale

creams and green, depicting seven children at a crumbling fence, trying to replace the fallen logs. The children are dressed in good clothing, as if they should be indoors. A flop-eared dog leaps the lowest
railing. A woman with a bundle of kindling over her shoulder and
with hand on hip stands smiling at the young people. She approves of
their labor. In the background are firs and a waiting horse. Everyone
seems to be working together happily, mending a piece of fence in the
middle of a field. On a moment's reflection, one's perception changes:
The children's features are indistinguishable; their proportions are just
a little off; the mother isn't toiling; someone unseen has arrived. It isn't
at all a happy scene.

I organized class notes and wrote up new assignments. The
building stirred with returning students. I was glad to hear them.

I had three interruptions—phone calls—that day. The first was
Justinia. She was failing a humanities course and had tried, before
the break, to arrange some satisfactory out.

"He's unreasonable. I had to read four hundred pages a week. I
got behind."

"Take an incomplete."

"He won't give me one. He says an incomplete would mean I've
missed only one major assignment. He says I've done them all, but
just poorly."

"That's probably the rule in the *Student Handbook*."

"Would you talk to him?"

"No."

"Why not?"

"It's not appropriate. You should ask to meet with him this week
and explain that you know you haven't done well. Tell him you've
been working all semester and have had some personal problems.

You could even go to the Student Affairs office and explain the situation. Someone will help you."

"But *you* won't."

"I just have. I've given you good advice."

"One phone call, and I wouldn't have to tell anybody anything."

"That's likely untrue."

"I haven't asked you for anything. Except a ride. One time I asked you for a ride."

She was right. I conceded.

"If you want me to phone him, I will. But it will be my head on the block. Is that what you want?"

After a heavy pause and a sigh, an attempt to persuade, she said, "I guess not. But if none of this stuff works, it'll be on your shoulders."

"All right."

"Could I borrow a copy of your book?"

"What for?"

"To show a friend."

"You mean to buy your passage out of the problem. No."

"Bye, Bloomin' Arthur."

She was coming into adult female form. But I was *amused*. She wasn't a dangerous version.

When the phone rang again, I assumed it was Justinia, renewing her argument.

"There you are!"

Grace. She came from such a distance that I couldn't remember when I had last thought of her. Surely only a day or so. Her words, those three particular words, reminded me how forceful she was, and how she viewed me.

"Right where you left me. Where else?"

"You should have come with me," she said. "Even bad weather is better away from Mason."

"You could probably stay gone, if you really wished to. You can afford not to work." I carried the phone into the kitchen, turned on the burner under the teakettle.

"That's a misconception some of my coworkers have. Anyhow, I'm not that sorry to be here. Home is home. Facing the darling students is what I really dread, especially with spring on its way. Their blood warms up faster than their brains. You want to come over? We could make my transition a little more pleasant."

"I shouldn't. I haven't been well the past few days."

"Then you need comforting. Please come. I'll take care of you, keep you warm."

"I'm warm enough. I think I'm feverish. I was just mixing up tea and lemon, and I need a good night's sleep. You probably do, too. I bet you've been burning your candle at both ends."

"That's what holidays are for. And while I may need it, I don't want it. I'm even willing to come over there."

"Really?"

"Yes. I've been a snob, I think. Maybe worse than that."

"I'm glad to know I'm acceptable now."

"You were always acceptable. You just weren't . . . "

"Acknowledgeable?"

A decent pause. "That'll do. I'm sorry. I've been chastising myself."

"Good. Unfortunately, though, none of this cures a cold."

"Right. Okay. So I shouldn't come over?"

"You shouldn't come over."

"Sad little girl here."

"Sorry."

"All right. I'll leave you to mend alone. You *are* going in tomorrow?"

"I never miss work."

"Good for you. Not all of us are so dutiful."

There ensued a silence that I assumed was mine to fill, but I was at a loss for more to exchange.

She spoke up. "Didn't you *miss* me?"

"I still do."

"Well done. I'll see you tomorrow. Maybe." She hung up.

The third caller didn't speak. The silence was familiar. You can sense the force of a personality held in check. "Who is this?" I said gently. I heard a distinct draw on a cigarette, an intake of breath. Who else among my acquaintances smoked? Then the phone clicked.

Harper? Could he tell I had been in his office? Perhaps he did have a talent other than words.

⌒

I turned to Nada's pages at about six that evening.

I didn't know that I had expectations until I began reading. I wanted something beautiful, uplifting, so rich in love and life and longing that I could inhale it into my very bloodstream and keep it prisoner. The first entries were dated May 11, 1935, and that was the most engaging detail. She would have been twelve or thirteen. She wrote of proud tulips and Sweet Williams and the thieving crow. There was a hint, though, of something working beneath the words, drawing her along. And drawing me. She wrote about an oriole that could not sing without honey and a young boy who ate the honey in hopes he could sing; about a young girl who could not tat lace and exchanged her supper for another child's tatting; a girl who grew so fat she cut strips from the center of her petticoat and sewed them into the waistband to extend it and add space between seams. She couldn't hang the petticoat up to dry, so she washed it by hand at night and often wore it wet. She wrote a short piece about a dog being bludgeoned to death by a young boy, a longer piece about turtles whose legs had been chewed off by the family dog.

In the second volume, I found a character, a young woman named Rose, about thirteen years old. She was in a convent. She had a mirror small enough to conceal in the palm of her left hand. During the day, she kept it beneath her clothing, though at times it caused her severe discomfort. Once it cut into her breast and she feared the droplets of blood would reveal her secret. She pressed her finger to a thorn and let that account for the slight red stain on her white smock. A few "precious times" she found herself alone long enough to try to catch glimpses of her face, but she couldn't "capture her entire visage at once." One night, she disrobed beneath the blankets and attempted to view her naked body in the small fragment of glass, but she could see only white smooth skin, and not how the entire being came together. The mirror fell from her clothing one day, and one of the sisters in the convent took it away. Rose, "the fair beauty, paid penance."

It was an outdated romantic piece, but touching, and might have been publishable during the time it was written, if she had been wise enough to try or had had a mentor. I could visualize the character. Of course, I saw a young Nada, and that made me a little sad. But I hadn't harmed young Rose and never would.

I glanced ahead to assure myself that Rose appeared later. I was glad to have the story waiting for me. I went on to bed. I went to sleep easily. I admit I wasn't racked by guilt. Nada was seventy-three years old, and nobody cared more for her than I did.

⌐

A farmer named Ernest Hollowell found Nada Monday morning. He was clearing the road from his farmhouse to the highway and first saw her car. Then he saw the body. He went down the embankment on foot because he thought she might still be alive and need help immediately, but when he realized she was, as he said, "stone-cold dead," he finished clearing the last few yards of road and then went back to call the sheriff. I liked Ernest. He was the epitome of Missouri practicality. He was also respectful of the subject and situation. He never smiled and he didn't slip into that low-register, spaced-words voice so many people use when they think they're in the middle of a tragedy and the world is watching. He was just himself and that was good enough.

Although I had no morning class to meet, I went to the office at about ten, because it was the time of year when students begin appeals for favors, such as the one Justinia was preparing. They need new copies of the syllabus, extra credit assignments, or permission-to-drop-with-no-grade. I'm amenable to what will help young students. A few truly hard-luck kids might come in early. As I unlocked my own door, I saw a queue along the wall outside Harper's. I couldn't advise them how to handle him other than to be brilliant and disciplined.

Grace often had a television on in the morning, but only for a voice in the house. She was fond of old movies, especially from

works she had taught. So she hadn't seen Mr. Hollowell on television. Margaret told her. I can only visualize the hog-eyed pleasure
in her telling. I saw Grace's reaction. She came into my office
stunned, staggering. With hand on door, to chair, she managed to
sit down, leaving the door wide open.

"Have you heard, Arthur?" she said, in a guttural voice. "My
God. Did you hear about Nada?" She was blanched white, her red
lips garish.

I came around the desk and shut the door. I put my hands on
her shoulders and leaned down, whispered. "I saw it on the news as
I was leaving. I hoped I'd get to you first."

"It was Margaret. She just blurted, 'Did you hear about our
Nada?' She's a sick woman, Arthur. I want her fired."

"I don't blame you."

"God," she said, "God. To have a *stranger* find you. Lying in the
mud, and then a *stranger* comes along."

I wanted to tell her there *was* no mud on Sunday. The world was
frozen. But of course I couldn't.

"You should have called me," she said, "or come by the house.
Damn. I hate that Margaret. I can't get her nauseating, smug, slimy
tone out of my head. I want to *hit* her." She raised her right hand.
"With this. I want to smack that look off her face."

Grace's agitation didn't pass. She couldn't sum up the sorrow
and move on. Billy Butler came up to my door and she waved
him away.

"I should probably talk to him," I said. "I'll be right back."

I hurried down the hall. "Billy! What's up?"

"I wrote a new piece over break and wondered if I could turn it
in this week."

"Excited about it, are you?"

"I think it's pretty good. I know it's not my turn."

"We'll get it in. Put the copies out on the counter."

He held up a folder. "I happen to have copies right here."

When I went back, Grace wasn't in my office. I found her in the main office, talking to Margaret in clear, angry tones. "So, no more announcements like that, you hear me? You represent this department as long as you're being paid by us, and you either keep your mouth shut or speak respectfully of Nada. And wipe that supercilious expression off your face this minute or get your disgusting self out of the building."

Margaret scurried around her end of the counter and into her boss's office. The door shut. I could see the phone. A button lighted up.

"She'll call the dean," I said.

"Good. I hope she calls the president, the newspaper."

I took her elbow. "Let's go back to my office."

"No," she said. "A *student* might come in."

She stalked away, toward the lounge, then stopped. I came up to her.

"I should have ignored him," I said. "He's just one of my favorites."

"They're all your favorites." She sniffed. Her face was flushed. "But that's not a bad trait." She looked down the hall at Harper's waiting line. "That's the bad trait."

She turned toward the lounge and I went with her. I had come so I could be in my office, but that wasn't to be. At least I had been available for Billy, who waved at me as he left our floor.

Dr. Walsh, arriving, saw us and came into the lounge.

"I guess you've heard," he said, "about Nada."

"Yes," Grace said, "from our slug-faced receptionist. I want to talk to you about her."

"Now?" He was obviously reticent to do so, but alarmed by Grace's tone.

"No. Let her give her side first."

"All right." He glanced at me as if I would explain Grace. She looked a little less pathetic, though still miserable. Her face had regained a more natural color, but the tip of her nose was pink and mascara had smudged a half-quarter moon beneath one eye.

"Why don't you cancel classes, Grace?" he said. "In fact, maybe we should all do that. It's appropriate."

"Not the day after spring break," I said.

He looked from me to Grace and back.

"Right. I guess not. I know. We'll make it optional. I'll tell Margaret to expect a lot of cancellations. She can post notices." He left the lounge.

Grace, eyes still moist, said, "Arthur, come on . . . "

"I can't just cancel classes. I'm not in your position. I take my work very seriously."

"Yes, you do. But what about everything else?"

"I do what I can. The best I can."

She shook her head, as if dispelling a weak shudder. "Of course you do," she said. "We all do." She went to look out the window. "I had a miserable night," she said. "I hoped you would change your mind and come over."

"I wouldn't have been good company."

"You *could* have been. Colds aren't the end of the world." She turned around, found a cigarette in her purse, and lit it—a gesture of defiance against policy, if not against fate. "By the way, what happened to that cold? You look in the peak of health to me."

"I stayed home and took care of myself. I can't afford to be sick this time of year."

She nodded, took another drag, exhaled. "I should have checked on her. I could've called last night or this morning. I could have offered to pick her up."

"It might have happened before you got home. Did the news say?"

"I don't know. It doesn't matter now. I don't want to know if I could have made a difference. It's too late."

"You should go home. Do as Dr. Walsh suggested. Cancel classes. Be kind to yourself."

"I want company. Come with me?"

"I can't."

"Why?"

"You know why."

She snapped off her list of charges: "Because you must meet your students and fill this day like you fill them all, with your *schedule, work, duties*. No grand passions for you."

I waited for her to run down.

"You're not going to cancel classes, are you?" she said.

"No."

"Of course not." She went to the sink, ran water on the cigarette, and dropped it in the trashcan.

I left the lounge and returned to my office. Billy had laid a copy of his story in the middle of my desk. I put it in the appropriate stack. His submission didn't come first.

Grace came to my doorway. "I'm sorry," she said.

"That's all right."

"I'm just getting after you because I feel so bad."

"I know."

"I really am sorry. Forgive me, okay?"

I nodded, but without looking at her. In a few seconds, she left.

I went into the hallway, and when I found the lounge empty, entered it. I stood by the windows for the dense, almost solid cold near their surface. I wanted to press my face against the glass but didn't want anyone seeing me do that.

The strength and vehemence of Grace's reaction to Nada's death disarmed me. She had consistently belittled Nada, even degraded her, yet now she adopted anger and grief as appropriate—or genuinely felt those emotions.

What did Grace feel for me? How would I ever know if it had to be shaken out of her by something like death?

I went to my office. I was ashamed of Paul Harper. Two of the waiting students had had to leave, presumably for classes.

Grace returned to my office. She leaned against the jamb, arms folded. She had removed the smudged makeup, but her eyes were swollen, the skin beneath them a translucent blue. After a moment, she turned away. I heard the light clomp of her boots recede as she walked down the hall. Then the sound stopped. She was reconsidering. I heard her coming back.

Women have a way of doing that, circling, false starts. They do it in conversation, too.

She appeared in the doorway. "Will you come by after class?"

"You want a part of my little life? Yes. I'll come by."

"I said I was sorry."

"All right."

"If you cancel your classes, we could go to the city."

"I'm not fond of the city."

"But you will come by?"

"Yes. If it will make this easier."

"I don't want it to be easier. I want to hurt for her. What time will you come?"

"Four-fifteen."

She glanced around my office, overtly noting all the artifacts of Nada. "Do you actually *care* about students that much?" she said. "They wouldn't care if *you* had died, or me, or the president, or God, as long as their little papers had an A. They're greedy, egotistical, sniveling, . . . " She seemed to hear her own voice and, shamed as she should be, moved away from it.

But she didn't leave, so where was the truth? What she really believed was that if *she* went home, we all should, and we weren't obeying. For the next half-hour or so, I heard her voice here and there as she talked to others.

Who can add anything to what they are? What's made is made is made.

I cancelled my classes after all, because Dr. Walsh suggested that the whole department do so. It was better to present a uniform respect than to let some professors appear callous.

I wrote my own note:

> Mr. Blume's classes are cancelled for today.
> Please direct any questions to the office secretary.

I went home until four and mulled over Grace's pain. Then I drove to her house. She was no longer crying, but she didn't look well.

"I've taken too many pills, I guess," she said. "I'm dizzy and a little nauseated."

"Do you want me to go home?"

"No," she said firmly. "Stay with me, if you can bear it. I'll try not to be too intolerable."

She wanted to recount the news she had heard, and I listened, observing her reaction. She was feeding her own grief, but I didn't tell her so. She wouldn't have been receptive. She fixed us strong coffee and put an old movie in the VCR.

It was a classic film, a black and white titled *The Witness*. A fat old guy, married to a harridan, sacrifices his morals, his reputation, and his security to save a young wife from a brutalizing alcoholic husband.

We didn't make love. Grace never made a gesture in that direction. Grace said, "Why did you like Nada? What did you see in her?"

"An older woman with dreams and ambition."

A few scenes later, she replied, "I think it was more than that."

"Do you?"

"Do you, *Grace*," she said.

I let that pass.

"Were you ever at her place?" Grace asked. "Her little box of treasures?"

"No."

"Why not? She invited everyone."

"I was invited, but the time never came."

She wanted me to spend the night. She slept fitfully, moaned often. The room was too hot and there were too many covers. I sat in the living room for a while, nude, and when I stood to return to the bedroom, my ghost reflection filled the black television screen.

The torso was burly, the legs spindly. My future? My old man body? Somebody else?

⟵

Nurturing sounds are supposedly universal, across species, so we recognize comforting sounds, sad ones, threatening ones, mews and growls, roars and screams, lows and brays, coughs and grunts, chirps and screeches. Hisses. Who would know to run from a whispered endearment?

Other women have advised me that saying a woman's name is a crucial part of intimacy. It doesn't do just to say "there you are," "how are you," "I brought these for you." It's the name that creates reality. A vase can't be a vase until one calls it exactly what it is. A rose, a rose, a rose.

⟵

I went home in the dark early morning, showered, dressed for work. A newscast had more clips, shots of an ambulance, of the sheriff, of a surprisingly small mound under a sheet. The camera zoomed down on the pink ribbon just at the edge of the sheet, and then fanned up and away to a black skeleton branch of a winter tree.

Nada, Nada, in the cold, tell me how your garden grows.

At the appropriate time, I went to the office. Now colleagues stopped and exchanged a few sentences about Nada, shook their heads, spoke in hushed voices. It's part of the ritual that makes the living feel safe, paying respect to the dead.

Grace didn't come in that day, Tuesday. The cancellation note remained on her door.

At mid-morning, workmen from the physical plant appeared. They installed an extension of the counter around Margaret's work space. It was a padded partition, gray and about six feet tall. It blocked off the side and back of Margaret's area. No one could thus approach her except over the counter or around the farther end. It was quite ludicrous. Grace was half the size of Margaret. Of course, surprise is always an advantage. Some people, without surprise, could vault the counter.

I met my classes, followed my syllabus. I suggested they begin thinking of a fair format for a final exam. They could even suggest a percentage of the questions.

Paul Harper stopped by my office before I left. "I'm going to miss the old girl," he said. "She was at least interesting."

"Yes, she was that."

"Do you think it was really an accident?"

"Of course. Why would anyone think otherwise?"

"She didn't drive in weather like that. Something got her out."

"What did she have that anyone would want?"

"Beats me," he said, and shuffled out of my office.

⟿

There was no message from Grace in my mailbox or on my recorder. She wouldn't have left a message with Margaret, and if she had, the creature wouldn't have passed it on to me. I found the lack of contact odd, but I didn't call Grace. I was willing to stay with her as long as she needed, but I was relieved to have free time, even a small amount. Manuscripts were awaiting me at home.

⟿

Nada had been raped at some time in her life. I gathered that because her character Rose had been raped. Nada disguised the incident by setting the story in a past time and another country (British flower gardens, rock walls, rain, fog, etc.), but I think the incident itself occurred about the way she described it. Rose, the girl of the mirror in the earlier piece, is in love with a boy named Stephen, "who helped the stone mason." They plan to marry but, like many young people, get carried away. One day shortly after their spring-field dalliance, Rose descends into the convent cellar to "fetch potatoes."

Her free hand held the thick folds of her black skirt, so she might see where she placed her small feet. Rose didn't care for the cellar. The dank smell and heavy shadows offended her nostrils and eyes, and quickened her heartbeat. She was a dutiful child, though, cheerfully obedient to every Sister's request. She whistled a little tune as her slippers reached the dirt floor, but she didn't yet release her skirt. She eyed the floor and shelves suspiciously, craned her delicate neck to peer beneath the stairs. She feared rats and snakes, spiders, all the denizens of dark recesses. The potatoes lay in heaps against the far wall and, still whistling, Rose moved slowly in that direction. She was very wary because, though she was never comfortable in the cellar, this afternoon she was even less so. She felt that something watched her, something not good at all.

She chose the potatoes hastily, without turning her back completely to the stairs and the odds and ends stored beyond them. Once she was certain of a movement there, behind a lopsided bureau, and she paused, holding her breath for a short time.

"You just go away," she whispered. "Whatever you are, old rat." She watched closely but nothing moved again, and she filled the basket quickly, standing and turning to run across the room and up the stairs. But she never did run. Because there, standing just at the bottom of the stairs, was the gardener. He had shears in one hand, and his crushed hat in the other.

"How do, missy," he said.

Rose was afraid. She had reason to be. He dragged her behind the stairs. He ripped the soft cloth that covered her breasts. She was ashamed.

"Take off your clothes," he said. He pressed the sharp points of the shears against her breast.

Rose did as she was told to do. She didn't struggle. She cried out, but not loudly. She didn't want to die and she was very ashamed that she didn't want to. She closed her eyes once but thought then he would kill her certainly, and she opened them again.

When he finished with her, he didn't let her leave. He sat on the dirt next to her and toyed with her body. He traced the shears everywhere. Rose never said, "Don't." He told her which way to move her limbs. Then he said, "Get your clothes on." He watched her dress. "Turn around," he said. He brushed dirt from her skirt and she was stunned at her gratitude for the gentle gesture. He walked to the stairs. "Pick up them potatoes," he said, "and go about your business."

Rose tells no one. She completes her chores for the evening, peeling the potatoes, setting the table. She pretends to eat. The next morning, she sees from her window that the gardener still occupies the same world as she.

And so the story goes—Rose sends Stephen on his way. She's too shamed to "live in his pure love." When she "swells with child" and is found out, she does penance. At night she holds her belly and "wonders at the child within, angel or monster?" She determines that if the child is fair like Stephen, she will not let "heaven nor earth take it" from her side. But the child is born with "skin the hue of cellar soil" and she cuts a lock from his hair but lets him be taken away. She leaves the convent a year or so later, to "find work that would purchase her freedom from shame."

Had Nada had a child? Perhaps. But I never once entertained the thought that I was that child. That would have been ridiculous. Someone else thought of that possibility and the press has made it mine. I wouldn't propose something so patently false.

I would have continued reading until I finished every volume, but I was again interrupted. When I heard the knock and started toward the door, the thought came to me that it might be Jack. For just a few seconds, I anticipated talking with him. And why not? We shared a tragedy. One had come among us.

But instead of Jack, I saw Grace, a different version of Grace. She wasn't in the right place. And she didn't look like the Grace I had learned to deal with. She wore no makeup and was dressed as if she had been running—jeans, blue sweatshirt, brown leather jacket, tennis shoes, and a brown leather cap. She looked like someone who was trying to appear tough, like a boy, but she couldn't pull it off.

"Could I come in?" Her husky voice cracked, as if she might cry.

"You certainly may."

I didn't know what to do with her. I thought perhaps she had come for the intimacy we had neglected the night before. I thought this was female to male, Grace to Arthur. I stepped close to kiss her cheek and she withdrew, overtly and sharply.

"I've been really rough on you," she said, with a glance toward and past me. "I'm sorry." She walked into the living room, remained standing as she looked around.

"You've been under stress," I said.

"Yes, and I still am. I took a pill." She pushed her hands into her pockets. "Actually, I've taken three of them again today. I haven't been able to find an even keel. I feel wrenched around."

"You're letting it get to you. You can't change it."

"No. But I can confront it and feel guilty about it."

That sounded right to me. Admirable. She had her moments.

Her gaze again swept over my apartment. "This isn't what I expected, not at all."

"You thought I'd be more spartan."

"Yes, I did. Your taste is a little like Nada's."

"Many people like Victorian furniture. Let me take your coat. I'll get you some coffee."

"Coffee would be good. I'll keep my coat on, though. I can't get warm. I've been this way since I heard about her."

"That's normal for you. You can't ever get warm."

She sat down on the sofa, tight as a coil.

I went into the kitchen, took down cups, and filled them. A slight sound or something urged me to look into the living room. She was no longer on the sofa. I went after her. She was in the hallway, coming toward me.

"I tossed my coat on the bed," she said. "All right?"

"Of course."

"It's probably not a good idea to keep it on in here. Then I'll freeze when I go outside." She followed me into the kitchen. "I need lots of sugar."

I put the sugar bowl next to her cup and handed her a spoon. She put in four heaping teaspoons. Her hand trembled and she spilled sugar on the counter and sloshed coffee onto the saucer. I got a bigger cup and poured her coffee into that.

"Do you have any napkins?" she said. "Give me a handful."

I carried the cups into the living room. She sat down, lit a cigarette. "You'll let me smoke in here, right?"

"Yes." I slid a small dish toward her.

"That's not an ashtray."

"It can be washed." I still didn't know why she was here.

"I've said so many ugly things about Nada," she said. "I can't bear to think of them. It's all going to come back on me someday, when I'm older. We pay, Arthur. We don't get to be vile creatures and get out unscathed."

"You're not a vile creature."

She drew deeply on the cigarette. "Yes, I am."

She was looking so fiercely at me just then that I suspected her words were meant for me. That she was really saying, "Yes, you are."

"You're not angry with me?" she asked.

"Never."

"That's good." She drew on the cigarette again, and suddenly stood up. "Bathroom's in the other bedroom?"

"Yes. Let me show you."

She was quick, up and heading to the bedroom, where I had been reading, where Nada's work lay on the bed.

I came to the doorway. Lamplight fell on lined paper slipping from the folders. I pushed the pages back, stacked the folders. The bathroom door was open. Grace had removed her cap, and stood before the mirror, fluffing up her hair. "I look terrible," she said. She turned on the faucet, bent down, and rinsed her face. She dried it with a hand towel, turned around. "I'm sorry I've barged in on you."

"I'm glad to see you."

She came out, glanced at the bed. "You were working, I see."

"A little. I can't concentrate either."

She passed me, probably full of trepidation, but willful anyway, determined.

She talked about her responsibility for dealing with Nada's final business, having to find addresses of family and friends, looking for a burial dress. Although she talked clearly enough and remained seated, she hadn't really calmed down. She had crossed her legs and locked the toe of one shoe behind the chair leg. She steadied her cup by holding her left palm beneath it. And when she brought the cup to her lips, she didn't actually sip any. There was a fine tremble in her lips when she tried.

I told her she needn't try to handle all Nada's personal details.

"Someone has to do it," she said.

"It doesn't have to be you."

"Yes, it does."

Then came *the* question, the one that in retrospect explained all her painful restraint. "Do you have any of her notebooks?"

"No. Why should I?"

"I know she wanted you to read her work. She gave you one. I thought you might have others."

"No. I planned to read her manuscripts when I could, but I haven't had time."

"I thought maybe you had planned to read them over spring break."

"No. That was Loeffle. He told her he'd get to her poems then. Have you talked with him?"

In total, she stayed about an hour. Perhaps she thought time alone would advise her what to ask or do next. I didn't attempt to sit by her. That was her choice. I was following her cues. Outside my window, the night coasted by, high black skies, white-light stars, crisp winter wind.

I walked her to her car and offered to follow her home.

"No, thanks," she said. "I can manage alone."

I put my arms around her and kissed her forehead. She had put her hand on her cap, to keep it in place, and she didn't kiss back. She didn't tremble either. I think she only endured my touch, perhaps as a leave-taking.

I didn't know then what she had been doing.

⟜

In disposing of Nada's writings, I stumbled onto another strand of the pattern.

I placed the folders in manuscript boxes, and secured them together with heavy twine. Under the top knot, I inserted a sheet of paper with my mother's name and address. Then I put the bundle into a large box, wrapped it in brown mailing paper, and addressed it to my mother but at an old address of mine. I put no return address at all. So, when the box was delivered, it would be returned to the post office. Of course, someone might accept the box, open it, and just destroy what appeared to be worthless personal papers. But if routine ruled, as it usually does, the box would be returned to the post office. There it would sit, since it could not be delivered. A few notices to the address would be mailed. Eventually—months, even a year or more—the box would be forwarded to another station or it would be opened. If they contacted the internal address, they would either receive no information or would learn that the addressee was long deceased. They would then, perhaps, destroy the contents. They might attempt to ascertain the whereabouts of any survivors. If so, the box might, only might, find its way back to me. I could, of course, claim the box during all this time, because I knew its destination and addressee. I could request a trace. In any case, either I would receive the manuscripts or they would be destroyed. Either I ended up with Nada's stories, or no one did.

The next morning, I drove sixty-five miles to mail the box from a large post office in Kansas City, one so busy that I had to take a number and wait my turn. The postal clerk didn't notice, or at least didn't care, that there was no return address. He said, "Do you want to insure this?" I said, "No." I paid the fee and left.

Along the highway back to Mason, red-winged blackbirds darted. It was an amazing flock, stretching thin for miles. They had to be all males, the uglier females off somewhere or not arriving. They have harems, these blackbirds, and fend off challenges that the females enticed.

CHAPTER 23

MASON, SPRING 1992

I'm a voracious reader, as was my mother. I owe her for that. And I'm eclectic. Maybe I even prefer fact to fiction. I enjoy Frazier, Campbell, Girard, Freud, Foucault, Gould, Sagan, Thomas, Asimov, Eiseley, and the like. An interesting world is an interesting world.

Serial killers are not supposed to have a sense of smell, at least not a keen one. That's why they often don't detect the stench that warns their neighbors, why they are able to drive around with a decomposing body in the car. They retain artifacts to help them remember exactly what they need and want to remember. They do not hate their victims but often love them. They enjoy the game. They want to get caught. They want to be stopped. They also want to continue their habit forever and ever. They *know* they're sick, or, more accurately, they know they differ in some grand way from others. They make good neighbors. They are mild people. Sometimes their violence astonishes them. They would like to understand. They have a pattern, a modus operandi.

At this moment, I'm tempted to draw one of those little smiley faces women like to draw, to take the sting from a word.

They know, too, that there may be gaps in their thinking, the cause of the genuine "I don't know." Everybody in the world wants to identify patterns in sufficient time to be safe. Suppose the pattern is one's *own*, but painstaking attention will not reveal it? It's like trying to find a shadow in darkness.

A defensive method is, as I've at least suggested, to copy.

The best defense is randomness.

Random is as random does.

⌒

Wednesday morning, when I entered the department lounge, Grace and Carl Loeffle were quietly talking before the wide, cold windows. Dried leaves from the lounge ficus were on the floor around their feet. She looked directly at me, with an expression I could not identify. It certainly wasn't fondness or pain or anger or even courtesy or recognition. Perhaps it was approaching contempt, which I hadn't earned. She had wanted something perfectly suited to her needs, but supplied on demand. I guess. There was a touch of Nada about her, a certain cast in the eyes.

Suspicion?

"Arthur," Loeffle said, in his always friendly fashion. "Got a minute?"

"Sure."

On one of the round tables was a sheet of typing paper with a message in large red-ink letters:

> Donations for flowers for Nada Petrovich should be
> given to Margaret by 4:00 p.m. today.

I sat down at the table to write a check, and Carl pulled out a chair across from me.

"Grace and I have been talking about doing something special to recognize Nada. Do you have suggestions?"

I did, something that was appropriate and would speak well of all of us. Nada would have liked it, too. "Perhaps you could edit a small edition of Nada's poems."

"That's perfect. Grace?" He turned to look at her. "Did you hear that? Arthur says we might publish some of her work." He turned back to me. "Was she that good?"

"No. But the purpose wouldn't be to impress the literary world, would it? It would be in memoriam, a tribute."

"I think it's an excellent idea," Loeffle said.

Grace had come to the table. "So do I."

"Would you be willing to help?" Loeffle addressed me. "Grace says there are about sixteen notebooks of poems. It's a lot of reading. The poems would have to be edited, arranged. You know."

"I hate to say no, given the circumstances, and especially since I suggested the project. But I've read Nada's work, and wasn't too impressed. I liked her, but I'm not the right person for the job."

"Maybe you haven't seen her best efforts," Grace said.

"She selected the pieces."

"She may not have recognized her best work. *We* might. After all, we're trained for it."

She was observing me so closely I don't believe it mattered what I said. She wanted to look at me and listen to me, evaluating by some secret gauge. She was a bright woman, rather brave.

"You're right," I said. "I hadn't thought of it from that angle." I looked at Loeffle. "I'd be happy to help, but not to head up the project. Let me act as third reader. I'll read whatever the two of you pass on."

"That seems fair to me," Carl said. "We'll give it a shot. Maybe we'll have another Dickinson here."

"I don't think so," I said.

Carl left then, lanky and contented.

Grace remained standing by the table. She wore a red wool suit, black heels, and black stockings. A gold mesh bracelet encircled her left wrist. Her lipstick was as red as the suit. She was fortifying herself.

"Some of Nada's notebooks are missing," she said.

"Carl said you had sixteen of them. How many were there?"

"Sixty-two, I think, stashed here and there. Sixteen of poems, some of songs with key notations, many full of class and research notes, a few recipes, and twelve of I don't know what. Those twelve are missing."

"How do you know?"

"There was room for twelve on the remaining shelves."

"And the shelves have to be full?"

"You've been to her home. You know how she . . . "

I shook my head. "No. I don't know. I've never been to her house."

"The shelves were dusty. Books leave little imprints." With two fingers, she had drawn the outline of a long triangle. "Where the binders touch the shelf."

"Yes, they do that. And you think twelve are missing?"

"I know they are."

"I'll ask my creative writing students. Nada may have asked one of them to read her work. It would be like her."

Grace didn't respond. I glanced toward the hallway. "I wish you wouldn't be this way. I'm genuinely fond of you. I already miss you."

She turned away and walked back to the window. She had absolutely beautiful carriage, straight as a porcelain statuette.

"Why are you turning your back to me?" I said.

"I don't want to look at you. I know what you are."

⌐

When I left the building for lunch, I encountered the dean, Dr. Hirsch, who was just back from a meeting with the Provost. Fall enrollment was up, and the department would be advertising two new positions, in Women's Studies and American Literature.

"What about the tenure line for creative writing? Did it come through?"

"You don't have a terminal degree, do you?" he said, as if he didn't know.

"In creative writing, the MFA degree is considered terminal, and that's the degree I hold."

"They've decided it has to be a Ph.D., even in fiction. Or, if not, it has to be an affirmative action position."

"A woman."

"A minority. Or a woman. Sorry." He thrust his cigarette into the sand container. "We're under some pressure since our proportion is off. You'll be considered, though, Arthur. We wouldn't pull a low stunt like that. We were looking for a woman last year, in fact, but we advertised so late."

Paul Harper was approaching us with his sliding walk, his head forward like a straining turtle. He reminded me of Pope's apt description of a man "willing to wound but afraid to strike."

"Did you hear the latest about Nada?" he said as soon as he reached us. "They suspect," he indicated quotation marks with his fingers "'foul play.'"

The dean was now prepared to stay for a while. "Someone killed her?"

"They don't know for sure. But the news in the union said the wounds in her head were," he again marked a quote, "'inconsistent with a fall.'"

"Who would want to hurt her?" I said.

"Do they suspect anyone?" from the dean.

"Not yet." Harper raised one finger. "But the next installment is sure to come. Mason Monster." He laughed and glanced at me. "Crude joke, I guess," he said. "Well, life here offers little else." He went on into the building.

See? They had never planned to keep me at all.

⌁

The creative writing students wanted to talk about Nada. They were sincerely distressed, mindful of death, at least momentarily.

"Maybe," Sarah blurted, "we could get some of her poems for the student journal. What do you think? We could dedicate an entire issue to her."

"I think it would be a wonderful tribute. You should speak to Dr. Burch about it. She may offer to help."

With unusual reticence and somberness, they discussed the submissions for the day. They were kind to one another. Jack Goff sketched in the margins of the handout, then on the blank backside. He was drawing each of us. Nada was there, too. From his pen she was a little dumpling face.

Billy's new piece came last. It was fifteen pages long, which was over the maximum, unless a student requested permission to exceed the limit. He had not mentioned the length, but then I had not asked.

He was a model student writer. He listened to their criticism; he took notes. He made no response other than to flush when Jack said, "I wish I'd written it. It's that good."

It was about a carnival and a kid who had spent most of the evening trying to win a stuffed toy. While the carneys were loading up, he sneaked into the game tent and stole the prize he'd been unable to win. He left a quarter to pay for the chance he took.

Jack was right. Billy's eyes were alight with success and with a skill acquired. I had no doubt he had lived the story he wrote, if not in fact, in his dreams.

⤺

I had been home no longer than thirty minutes when someone knocked at the door. I recognized him immediately. Patterns are astonishing, even when you expect them. Deputy S. Dyer. Shirley Dyer. Huge, friendly, he was truly apologetic for the intrusion. "I'm talking to everyone," he said. "Just general questions, you know, about Miss Petrovich."

"You don't remember me? We met the day I arrived in Mason."

"That's right. I thought you looked familiar. This is nasty business, isn't it?"

"It is."

He wanted no coffee or tea, but he accepted a glass of water and looked for a coaster on which to place it. I appreciated that. I provided him one.

"There's been some talk about notebooks," he said. "Do you know anything about them?"

"I know Nada kept all her records and work in blue notebooks."

"Do you happen to have any of them?"

"No. I don't. I did have. Just one. She wanted me to read some of her poetry and I did so. But that was returned long ago, before class one evening."

"Okay. So you don't have any now?"

"As I said, no."

He nodded, sipped from the glass. He had hammy hands, with dark hair above and below each knuckle and on the backs. I wondered if his fingers would fit in the circle of a trigger. I've never handled guns of any kind.

"Would you mind if I looked around? You don't have to let me. I don't have a warrant or anything. But I'm supposed to check on the notebooks."

"Did someone think I may have them?"

"Actually, yes."

"And who might that be?"

"I shouldn't say."

I opened every door and drawer throughout the house, left them open for his Midwestern scrutiny—friendly and unrelenting. I even opened my file cabinet. "Feel free to look through the papers."

He was in the bathroom at that moment, reflected in the cabinet's triple mirror. He came out, looked in the closet, settled his attention on the boxes. "Could I look through these?"

"Yes. They're rejections of my second book. But feel free."

He lifted them down, seemed to consider sitting on the bed, then carried them into the living room and sat on the sofa. He took the lid from each, read the accompanying letters.

"Nothing here," he said, and carried them back to the closet. He returned to the living room, scanning the furniture with a turn of his broad, passive face, then smiling at me. "Could you tell me where you were last Friday?"

"I can't believe I'm a suspect here. But all right."

"It's standard procedure. We're asking everybody."

"It's difficult to remember, exactly. It was our spring break and every day was much the same. Let me think. Friday. Right. The ice. I was trying to beat a cold. I didn't want to leave the apartment at all, but I had to. I couldn't breathe well and couldn't stop coughing. I drove to Megamart. Or, rather, I slid to Megamart. They were just beginning to clear the streets."

"Yeah, that was a bad one." He hadn't written anything down. He took one more look around the room. "What about the rest of the day? What did you do?"

"Tried to get well."

"Okay." He smiled at me. "I guess that'll do. Thanks for the time."

"You're very welcome. I hope you find some answers."

I closed all the drawers and doors. I walked through the house scanning the surface of everything. Nothing. He couldn't have *seen* anything because nothing was there. In the bathroom, I studied my face. What would he have seen in me? Also nothing. A sad, older man's face, brown, large eyes dark and moist beneath brooding brows. I smiled at myself and the eyes lightened. A gentle man.

Patient. I returned to the living room and read for a while. Then I had dinner at my own table.

⌒

They arrested me the next morning. I answered the door and there was Shirley Dyer, sheepish but firm, and two other deputies. Shirley had a warrant and a small plastic bag. He went through the bedroom, into the bathroom.

"Yep," he called. "Still here."

He returned, holding up the bag. "Miss Petrovich's key," he said. "I saw it yesterday."

He was well suited to his work, appearing far less bright than he actually was.

CHAPTER 24

MASON JAIL, 1992

I wanted certain people to visit me that first week, particularly Carl Loeffle or some of my students. I wanted them to be shocked, to indicate by word or expression that they didn't believe the charge against me, that they couldn't believe it.

Grace did. She was dressed to the nines, as they used to say— hunter green dress and shoes, the latter with tiny curved heels and straps across her small, high arches; a light green scarf with a gold scarab at the throat; a delicate gold chain on her left wrist. Her bones were so small I could have snapped her into smithereens.

The visitors' room was long, narrow, divided its entire length by a counter with glass to the ceiling. We sat at the counter and spoke through receivers.

"I'm here," she clipped, "because I want to remind myself you're just a man, just Arthur Blume."

"I've been growing outsize, have I? In your imagination?"

"I keep remembering the times we were alone, how often I wondered what you were thinking. I was *way* off base. You were going to kill me, weren't you? You got sidetracked onto Nada. And there's more. I know there has to be." She paused, likely weighing whether she was prepared to say her next words. "Juliette Preston, for one."

She had hoped to surprise me, but I doubt that I registered the reaction she expected. After all, I had given her the name, freely, to play with as she wished.

"Don't frighten yourself and blame me."

"You didn't respond to what I said, Arthur."

"Yes, I did. You just want a different answer than the one I gave. That's always been the case."

"You haven't even said you're innocent."

"You haven't asked. And you haven't given me time."

"An innocent man would have been protesting the minute I got in here. He'd be threatening suit. He'd be . . . "

"I guess you've been an innocent man, and thus know exactly how one would behave."

She considered that. Then, "No. You're not going to play games with me. You did kill Nada and you were going to kill me. Still might, if you get out."

"I don't bear you any ill feelings, or wish you any harm at all. If you knew me, you'd know that's true. Stop worrying."

"I do know that's probably true. I also know you can't predict your own behavior. I've read the literature, Arthur. Some day, one year, five years, fifteen years from now, you could wake up and come after me. You might not even know that's what you're doing. Or what you've done."

"You think my word means nothing?"

"I'm saying I don't know what it means, and neither do you."

The glass between us was smudged. When Grace moved to her left, that side of her face was distorted. She might not have known it. But perhaps she leaned because the glass had the same effect on me.

"So I couldn't make you feel more secure, no matter what I said?"

"Even if you did, it would be false security."

"You could be right." She was a good thinker and I wanted to tell her so. "If I *did* say that I would never kill you, it might leave much open for interpretation."

She was watching me closely. She knew what I was about.

I continued. "Your retort might be that perhaps killing isn't *all* I could do."

She arose from her chair, and her voice was the guttural one. "I couldn't leave well enough alone, could I?"

"I would never hurt you. I was just explaining that I know how *you* think, too. We're both victims here, of conjecture. It's the creative mind that eludes understanding. And please don't leave yet. My students need help."

She didn't sit down, but she stayed. I asked who had taken over my classes, if she knew of my students' responses to the situation, what Carl Loeffle had to say. I told her where some graded papers were that needed to be returned to the students. "And there's a set of exercises in my apartment," I said, "for the next few assignments. They might cut the workload for the new instructor and give the kids some continuity. I don't want my professional work botched up over this."

"I hope you're one of a kind," she said.

In a pinch, we all fall back on clichés.

I know she still liked me, in spite of herself. I'm a pretty likable guy, or can be.

⟵

Justinia, too, came. How could she pass this up? To have been the one-night stand of a man charged with murder? Oh, the glory of it.

It warranted wearing that blonde mass up in a crown with a black ribbon woven through.

She behaved fairly well, too. "I hope you're not mad at me," she said.

"No. You're a fond little memory."

"You need anything? They said I could send stuff, books, gum, candy, cigarettes."

"No. I'm pretty comfortable, actually."

"They've got articles about you in the paper every day."

"I may be on television, too. Not now. Later."

That gave her pause. Would she be interviewed? What would she wear? But she surprised me.

"I'm not going to come anymore if that's okay. They asked me out front what my relationship was, and I didn't want to say 'friend.' I think if I come back they might get the wrong idea."

"What did you tell them you were?"

"I made them print 'acquaintance.' They laughed, but I thought that was more honest."

"You're right. Absolutely. And no, you needn't come again."

"I still wish I had one of your books."

"I'll send you one. I'll write 'To my dear Justinia' in the cover. How's that?"

"I'd like that."

"I thought you might. I appreciate your coming, whatever the reason."

She was pleased with herself. And she did look charming. The officers out front must have been speculating about the old boy with the bald pate.

⌐

The third visitor was Paul Harper. His slate black eyes swept over me. His lips curled at the corners—truly curled, like wood shavings.

"I couldn't miss this," he said. "It's the most exciting thing to happen in Mason since I've been here."

"I expected you."

"No, you didn't."

"Even though I'm the most interesting thing happening in Mason?"

"Oh, right. Perhaps you did expect me. I've heard that you stole Nada's work. Could that possibly be true? Was she that good?"

"No. There would have to be another reason."

"Such as?"

"You tell me. You probably know as much about it as I do."

He snorted. He needed to be wearing a monocle, to have a European cigarette pinched between two fingers, to have an SS guard outside the door so he could inhale fear without soiling his skin.

"And what do you mean by that?" he said.

"Let me quote you something I read recently. In an old record."

He waited, head cocked to hold the receiver steady, eyes already partially hooded. "Please do."

I said the name of the young woman who had marched her protest into his very grounds, and quoted a few of her words: "He had a soft and sticky voice"; "the old slug."

His eyes closed. "So long ago. Oh, yes. I recall. A limited vocabulary, but a pretty girl." He smiled. "Every now and then one comes along."

"Even in the military, I imagine, but you were there so briefly, perhaps you didn't have time to find out."

He took his pulse, but I knew it had quickened—his cheeks flushed a darker red than normal. I continued. "What kind of missions are you completing during your forays? A call here and there? A peek? How far do you actually travel on the train?"

When he finally opened his eyes, he said, "Nada?"

"Yes. Though I think she took a wrong turn about you."

"What else did you find?"

"It doesn't matter. I removed the file."

He considered this, then dipped his head to me.

He was a repulsive man, but I liked the way he accepted the gift.

"May I ask you a question," he said, "since you know more about me than I do about you?"

"Ask away."

"Nada. Why would anyone kill her?"

"Why not?"

He laughed. "May I quote you?"

"No. Dr. Loeffle told me that Nada once kept your class arguing over one word. What was it?"

"Guess."

"Her name? 'Nada,' only as used by Hemingway?"

He indicated his appreciation with raised brows. "Good boy. We were discussing 'A Clean Well-Lighted Place' and the prayer offended her. She said 'Nada' couldn't mean no values, the lack of meaning, as long as she was the reader or the reader knew of her."

"Fascinating woman."

"Pity she died."

"Yes. It is. Truly."

He leaned back, waited. When I didn't speak, he did. "Do you need anything? Word passed and so on? I owe you a favor."

"I'm comfortable here, as well as can be expected. You might mention at the next department meeting that I apologize for any inconvenience."

"Done. And what about Grace?"

"Nothing. We've spoken."

"You're satisfied with that?"

"Yes. I'm very fond of her."

"I can see that. All right." He stood, again bowed slightly.

When he reached the end of the glass partition, I called out, "Burn one of your little incense sticks for me."

He raised one hand in acknowledgment. "I'll smoke a cigar for you."

⌐

Serial killers can usually list victims, tell where their bodies are, what they were wearing at the time of their death, the weapon, if any, involved. It's not wise, though, to remember such details. If I made a list of any kind, the items on it would not be alike in any significant way, except that they came to my attention.

⌐

Overall, my interrogators were amusing:

"You did go to the Petrovich house on Friday morning."

"I don't know why you believe that."

"We have evidence that you left the apartment house early in the morning, that you were in possession of items belonging to Nada

Petrovich, and that you disposed of those items sometime over the weekend, probably late Friday evening."

"Why should I believe you have such evidence?"

"You were very interested in the woman's writing, and large sections of her writing are missing."

"Yes, I was interested in her work. She was a student of mine. But no, I was not very interested. And I doubt any part of it is missing. You people expect more of her than she had."

One deputy, overweight and slack-lipped, leaned down and said right into my ear, "Did you kill Nada Petrovich?" I leaned back so I could meet his eyes.

"Why would I do that?"

"You can't say 'No,' can you?"

"Certainly I can, and easily. 'No.'"

"I mean you can't say, 'No, I did not kill Nada Petrovich.'"

"That's a tricky statement. With two negatives, it could actually mean, 'Yes, I did kill her.' You're a wily one."

He looked stupefied and got a cup of coffee while he rethought the matter.

And so it went.

My guard would have made a good valet. Once I heard his footsteps and I called out, "I'm using the commode. Please wait a moment," and he did so, not coming near my cell till I called, "Thank you." It was a matter of pride I couldn't ignore. You can be a murderer and still be a man. A certain dignity is expected at all times.

I was moved to the maximum security wing. There the schedule for prisoners pretty well matched my own. I rose early, ate early, and at 10:00 was ushered, along with two other inmates, to the day room. The other two watched television and quarreled over channels. When they asked me to play cards, I went along and played for a while. I knew better than to win or to quit playing from boredom. Some murderers have fragile egos. I managed to lose so often that when I said, "I'd rather not play anymore, since you gentlemen keep beating the hell out of me," they were pleased.

I had an upstairs room, and from my window I could view the landscape of Mason and its outskirts. Maybe any country looks better in springtime, but there's a softness about budding trees, and Mason became charming. The courthouse dome held the sky upside down and sometimes I watched the clouds moving both above and below, and the dome seemed like a cosmic merry-go-round. I could watch it till I felt hypnotized and peaceful. And I could see the statues. One cherub. One gargoyle. Of course. Same size, maybe twins.

Then came the late spring storms. They were fierce. No one had warned me about this trait of Mason. I no longer wanted a room with a window. I wanted out. My breathing would get so irregular that I would become lightheaded. My heart pounded like a character in Nada's writing.

Once, when I thought I'd shake apart, I called the guard.

"I'm uneasy in storms. Could I possibly return to the day room?"

"I'm sorry, sir. We can't break the schedule."

"Of course. I understand."

He left, and a few moments later I had to call him again. "Could I be assigned another room? One without a window?"

"You sure you want to give up your window?"

"Yes."

It was a democratic jail. He let the other two inmates decide if they wanted to change rooms. They didn't.

I only called the guard one other time. I asked him if he would talk with me for a while. He did so. He suggested I consult the doctor. "He might prescribe some pills to calm your nerves."

"It's not that bad," I said. "The lightning is unsettling. I've made too much of it."

I didn't want pills.

I kept my misery to myself from then on. I sat on the bed and endured the frenzy of my fear. It didn't abate. It would come again and again all my life and no one would ever believe it. "You?" they'd say. "You suffer?" Yes. Me. I. Suffer. Just like anybody else. And I have to handle it alone.

⟶

Animals starve while researchers take notes and film the creature striving and wasting away. In one video a rangy cub thrashed and lunged in a mountain stream, while fish darted away like ripples. The cub's eyes got wilder. It craved madly. It knew what to do but didn't have the precise moves, the positions. In another film a young polar bear grew weaker under bland blue skies. It swam from floe to floe and its spine cleaved the water like the keen edge of hunger. The overvoices were compassionate, but no one intervened. No one tossed the animal enough sustenance for even one day's comfort. That would have upset the delicate balance of nature.

Maybe Harper had a hunger instilled and no means to assuage it. Maybe he never felt even one loving touch.

I began this book while I awaited trial. I wrote only mentally, but meticulously. I even did some revision before I could ever type a word. I have a good memory.

CHAPTER 25

We have to grapple with the mystery of women. That's the way it was with my mother. Anything could bring her to mind: a sun-haze, the snip of scissors, a pan of hot water. After the visit when she had her spells, I didn't go back for a long time.

When I was forty-three, I had been searching and experimenting with ideas for the second book, but they wouldn't take shape, wouldn't come into being. My prose was lifeless and staccato, regard-less of subject matter or point of view. And my contract with that particular community college was ending. I was dangling again. They might, they said, offer me a contract in the fall, *if* enrollment allowed, *if* monies were available. I would have to wait until the last minute.

"We could," the chair said, "give you some summer courses."

"Creative writing?"

"Sorry. Lester Early's teaching those. But we always have com-position."

"No," I told him. "I have a book underway. I think I can finish it this summer."

"Then that's what you should do. I've always thought I could write a book if I could find the time."

I wanted to tell him that it isn't actually that you have to *find* time. It's something you have to latch onto, wing away with, burrow into, drown yourself in. It eats time, devours it. No, finding time wasn't the answer.

When the semester ended, I gave all my furniture to the Salvation Army, packed my books, typewriter, and clothing into a small trailer, and left for Georgia.

I arrived late afternoon the third week in May. It was a dry spring, already hot, and I felt my first misgiving when I turned onto my mother's road. The air hung too still. A dust cloud floated in a distant field. I suddenly felt I was going in the wrong direction, that I should turn around immediately. But that wasn't my way, and I plowed straight ahead.

Her car was parked next to the house. I pulled up behind it and sat for a few moments, waiting for her to appear on the porch. When she didn't, I turned off the motor and walked across her yard. The front door was open and I called to her through the screen door. There was no reply. I entered, called for her again. I felt expectant and fearful. I wasn't *afraid* of her. After all, I was a grown man. It was something else. A lethargy, a heaviness. Something descending on me.

In the living room, the two recliners had been placed back to back in the center of the room. Three kitchen chairs had been brought into the living room and were stacked before the large front window. On the top one, which was upright, rested a blue teapot holding a wooden spoon. The lid of the teapot was centered beneath the bottom chair. Cups, glasses, and plates covered the end tables. A sandwich lay on the windowsill. The contour lamps were in opposite corners, both turned inward.

I walked through the other downstairs rooms. They were sweltering. In her bedroom, the long curtains had been drawn open, then the ends lifted to the center and tied into a knot. I undid them, opened windows, but no breeze stirred. Books were scattered along one side of her bed and on the floor next to it. I lifted a few and read the titles—*Mystery Love, Demon Castle, Ruth's Curse, Shadows and Secrets, Moonmaid, Forest Cries*. A column of them, crowned by a pill container, rose before the dresser mirror. I read the prescription. Mary Blume. Twice a day as directed. It was full.

I gathered up the plates in the living room, carried them into the kitchen and washed them. I waited on her to appear, wherever she was. I was just putting away the last dish when, through the kitchen window, I saw someone in the field just south of the house. The woman's torso was grotesquely rounded, so bloated that the head seemed thrust backward for balance, and the limbs seemed ludicrously delicate, far too small to support the weight of the body. She leaned from side to side as she walked.

In a few moments, she came through the back door. "I knew it was you," she said. "I saw that car turn off toward the place and I said, 'That's Arthur, come home again.' So I headed back."

"Where were you going?"

"Down to see the creek. Got red as blood yesterday. It bubbled up. Spit rocks."

She had walked to the sink and splashed cold water on her face. She patted it dry with the kitchen towel. Her hair was thin, cut blunt straight at the jawline. Her cheeks were puffy. Her facial skin, no longer smooth, seemed pitted, especially at the temples, as if the pores had enlarged and blackened. A thin layer of black hair lined her upper lip.

"Changed, haven't I?" she said, and folded the towel, laying it on the edge of the sink. "Happens to women if they live long enough. Belle says I should get a perm. I may do it. You want something to eat? Some iced tea?"

"No. Nothing."

"I got to get rid of that creek. It breeds ugly things. They're crawling all over the place. Where'd you live last? Chicago? Well, quit staring at me. You've changed, too." She opened a tray of ice, dropped cubes in a glass, and ran one cube over her forehead. "I bought Chicago one time. It had a black suitcase in its hand." She tossed the cube into the sink. "You here for long?"

She poured tea. Crazy as a loon and pouring tea. I could have left right then. There was a ridge of fat just at the nape of her neck. "I thought I'd spend the summer," I said. "Perhaps longer."

"You lose a job?"

"I resigned. I thought maybe I could write here."

"You could take the upstairs. It gets hot up there. You know that, though." She walked into the living room. I followed her. "Devil comes in the window sometime. You will have to keep it shut." She sat in the recliner, pushed it back. She kicked off her shoes. Even her nails had thickened. She picked up one of the books, held it as if she might read, but she watched me instead.

"I'd pay you rent, of course," I said. "And buy my own groceries."

She nodded. "That'd come in handy. Nobody's leasing land from me now and I don't want to get into my principal. Eats it right up, if you start drawing on it."

"You're not well. Do you know that?"

"I'm all right. What'd you come home for? You going to hurt me?"

"When did I ever hurt you?"

She squinted, shielded her eyes as if the sun were glaring behind me. Then she turned away and began reading. I sat watching her till she suddenly looked up and raised her hand as if she might slap my face. Then I went for my luggage. When I carried in the typewriter, she said, "Don't you make any noise. No noise at all."

"I won't," I said.

She read until dinnertime. Then she walked barefoot into the kitchen and fried bacon and eggs. She fixed toast and buttered it. She put strawberry jam next to my plate. "Supper's ready, Arthur," she said. We sat down together. She was fine while we ate. She washed the dishes. She read for a while and I lay on the sofa, listening to her turn the pages. I watched her cross the room and go out the front door. I went after her.

"Can you hear that creek?" she said.

It was a white night—the full moon cast a pale glow over the fields. She stood clutching her arms and twisting.

"Let's go in," I said.

She didn't respond. I touched her arm and repeated my words. I did that six times. Then she turned and went inside with me. I took a pill from the container and offered it to her. She ignored it. She went in the living room and unstacked the kitchen chairs. Then she stacked them again. I waited till she was seated once more, in one of the chairs in the middle of the room. I sat across from her and offered the pill again. About two hours later she took the pill.

I went upstairs, not to my bedroom but to the other one, where the door would lock from the inside. I secured myself and lay across the bed. I heard her leave the house and return twice more before I fell asleep. The next morning she took another pill from me. When she walked, I followed her, not far behind. Once she turned and ran at me, flailing her arms as if to shoo me away. That evening she took another pill from me. Three days later, when I replaced the furniture, she left it alone.

When I had been there a week, she said, "Belle says I have to move into town and get someone to look after me."

"That's an excellent idea," I said.

"She says if I don't do it, someone will do it for me."

I agreed.

The next morning, during breakfast, she said, "I gotta fix the creek. I want you to come."

"All right. Any special reason?"

"I want to show you something. You can help."

I didn't believe her because her voice and movements were more deliberate now. The medication had likely slowed her down. But her eyes were crazy.

When we were some distance from the house, I walked backward, to see how it looked that day, that moment. It had a beauty, a wholeness. It was our house and everything around it was ours.

Before we stepped onto the creek bridge, she scooped up a handful of pebbles. The bridge slanted sharply upward. It had been built to span the widest point necessary after heavy rains. Now, the water level was low, just a few inches over the flat center stones. The larger ones near each bank were bare and jutting.

She stopped when we were above the water, dropped one pebble at a time straight down.

"You the one hurt Iva Sutton?" she said.

"What makes you ask that?"

She dropped another pebble. She was wearing a brown, beltless dress. It was zipped only to the middle of her back.

"One time," she said, "I found a squirrel on this bridge."

"Did you?"

She dropped another pebble. "It was still alive. Bottom half of it was skinned, top half wasn't."

I didn't respond.

"There was a girl got hurt over in Wilshire," she said. "You were visiting over there."

"More than one, I think. More than one girl."

She tossed the rest of the pebbles, dusted her palms against her dress. She walked on.

"Belle says someone's going to put me away if I don't do something."

She stopped again, now on the highest point of the bridge. She turned to face me.

"You're just like me," she said. "You know that?"

She took my hands. She placed them not over her heart, not as a plea to feel the beating, but lower, cupping them against her sagging, wasted breasts. There was no light in her eyes at all. I didn't know what she was going to do. I didn't know what she wanted. I don't know who she thought I was.

I pushed hard and quick, and she fell exactly backward and down. She didn't actually bounce. Her head hit a wide slab of limestone and it lay beneath her head like a flat pillow. She moaned. Her eyes were open.

"No, I'm not," I said. "I'm not like you at all."

I sat down on the bridge. Dapple light played over me, her, the water. Ripples began and dissipated. Her lips moved. I thought perhaps she wanted to go home, but it wasn't time. If I walked to the crest of the higher bank, I would see the hunters' shack and the narrow road cutting through the fields. Everyone could use the road. No one had ever come for me.

I walked home and fell asleep. When I woke, I missed her and went back to the bridge. It wasn't my mother down there. My mother had black hair and quick ways. This was an old hag. I went down and dragged the carcass out of the water. It was very heavy. I brushed the hair back, and pulled the soaking dress down straight. It kept clinging and I smoothed it with my hands. Her shoes had fallen off, but I didn't want to get back in the water. No telling what was in there. I sat by her because another change might happen. I didn't look at her anymore. When I couldn't sit still any longer, I moved away very quietly and walked up to the bridge, and crossed it toward home. When I got there I called the emergency number. I told them my mother had fallen and I thought she was dead.

I walked down to the turnoff to wait on the ambulance, so I wouldn't have to go back there alone.

⟵

During the next week, I learned that all the money—and it had been a large sum—was gone, all withdrawn in one fell swoop, in cash. I can see her, carpetbag in hand, swishing mad and fine into the bank, waging a private war, purchasing freedom or joy by one slash into her fantasy. But it was gone. No trace, no record.

She may have given it to Belle, the starling. Women want to leave legacies and have so little to give.

While looking for what couldn't have disappeared so quickly and totally, I found the few items that prompted the first chapter of this manuscript: the news clippings about my grandparents' accident, the court record on my mother's mental competence to keep me in her care. I found photographs, including those she had taken from me. I guess she thought better of my staring at the features of Tim Welker, that handsome neighbor. But I looked no more like him than I did my grandfather or Sutton. Perhaps they all stirred the concoction. They were all handsome men. All larger than I. I got dwarfed in some transference, at least in comparison.

Now I know what she *might* have done with the money. She might have mailed it to herself. The idea may not have originated with me.

CHAPTER 26

A murder trial in a small town draws most of the populace—at least those persons whose work allows them freedom. They pack the courtroom. The air hangs hot and heavy and the audience waits with bated breath for one more detail, one more drop of blood.

That's not the way it really is. Some people don't go at all. They feel interest in such matters is crude, smacks of the gutter. Yes, it does.

Carl Loeffle never attended.

Paul Harper was there, of course, wholeheartedly. Every day of the trial, he sat in the front row, his skull face deceptively impassive. I don't know how he covered his classes. Vacation time, perhaps. Sometimes he nibbled at cookies or ate a candy bar. He had a thermos with him, too. The trial was his entertainment. Or study.

I believed I would be set free. It was better to believe that than to believe I wouldn't. Freedom was as possible as imprisonment. I doubt anyone wanted me to be guilty. And if I *were* guilty, they wanted to find a way to understand me and thus forgive me. I think everyone would have been happy if the judge pronounced me guilty, exonerated, and free. Then we could all go about our daily business, with everyone justified and purified. We could have dived into the sordid and morbid and emerged clean and smiling. It would be a true baptism, and truly romantic.

On the witness stand, Jack blurted more than spoke, revealing his youth and nervousness. He was reserved, though, and not dramatic at all, as though he had nothing against this Arthur Blume personally and wasn't trying to impress anyone. He occasionally looked at me as he testified, matter-of-factly. He wasn't afraid of me—good kid—but he didn't like the situation. I thought he should see me *differently*, somehow, at least like water that was darker than he had known. But not Jack. No, Arthur J. Blume was just a teacher he knew slightly and didn't respect too much.

"I couldn't sleep," he said, "for coughing. So I was up most the night. I don't know what made me look out the window. I do that sometimes if I'm up early. Maybe I heard something. But I did see Mr. Blume getting into his car and it was about 7:00 a.m."

"You're certain it wasn't 9:00 a.m.?"

"I can read a clock. It was 7:00."

"Did you look out again, later in the day?"

A nod.

"And?"

"His car was still there, but there wasn't any ice on the hood."

"That seemed odd to you?"

"Not then. Later, after the police talked to me, I got to thinking that he'd driven pretty far."

"Did you see Mr. Blume again that day?"

"Yeah. I was going down for a Coke and he was coming up the stairs."

"How was he dressed?"

"He had on a coat and gloves."

"Was he carrying anything?"

"No."

"Could you describe the gloves?"

"Dark blue. Not leather. Cloth of some kind."

"You know that no gloves like that were found in the suspect's apartment."

"I heard that."

"But you're certain he was wearing them?"

"Yep. He'd worn them to class a few times."

"Why would you notice that?"

Jack shrugged. "Most the guys I know don't wear gloves. Unless they're working outside. Shoveling or something."

"Okay. Now. Did he say where he had been?"

"No."

"Did anything about him indicate where he had been?"

"No. Just outside."

"And how did you know that?"

"He had left tracks, on the stairs and the floor. I was barefoot and I stepped on a piece of ice, slush, and that made me notice."

"So he had definitely been outside."

"I said he had been."

Jack clipped that answer. Good boy.

"Could it have been someone else's tracks? This is an apartment house and others might have come and gone."

"They were clear, one-person steps. Maybe the caretaker had just mopped up. I don't know. But there was one set, coming from the door to the stairs."

"Okay. Anything else, Mr. Goff? Anything out of place? Unusual?"

"A piece of paper. Little piece of blue paper about this size." He made a circle with thumb and finger. "It fell."

See? I had known that night. My undoing.

"Why would you remember something like that?"

"It was blue. He had on blue gloves and the paper was blue. I notice colors. And besides," he leaned back, draping one arm over the back of the chair, "it wasn't there when I went back upstairs."

"And why would you notice that?"

"I just explained."

They were through with Jack. They were pleased with Jack. Jack could have cared less. He had work to do. He had a life to live. He walked out, gangly and finished. I thought there might be a final glance between us. No.

Then came Justinia. She wasn't on the stand long, but she made the most of it. She wore a pink wool suit and she lied. She confirmed, to all and sundry, in a subdued parody of herself, that I was not the man I seemed to be.

"He'd been after me for quite a while," she said. "And he was a famous man. I just sort of gave in. It was spring break and everybody else was gone, having fun. I didn't have the money to go. He likes young women. All of us girls knew that. He may like young men, too. You know."

I whispered to my attorney, "She's lying. Does that matter?"

He shook his head no.

"Call back Jack Goff. Ask him about me."

"It's not worth pursuing, Art. It doesn't have anything to do with the case. And he might make it worse. Suppose he agrees with her?"

"He won't."

"I think he might."

"Then put me on the stand."

"I will later."

They called in Billy Butler. He didn't actually shuffle into the room, but he had that effect, as if he were too embarrassed to hold his head up. When he took the witness seat, a smile played nervously on his lips. If he'd had a cap, he would have twisted it in his hands. He was rather winning.

He said I hadn't treated Nada fairly in class.

"I'm sorry, Mr. Blume," he stuttered toward me. "But we noticed it." He looked back at the prosecutor. "She talked to some of us about it. We all knew he didn't like her, wished she wasn't in the class. She wrote some good stuff, but he wouldn't give it much class time. We're supposed to be allotted equal time. And when she spoke up in class? You know, when we talked about each other's work? Whatever she said, he—Mr. Blume—got this funny look on his face."

"What do you mean, 'funny look'?"

My attorney's objection was overruled.

"Mr. Blume's face," Billy said, "went blank, like he wasn't seeing any of us. Like he had gone somewhere. It was spooky." He shrugged. "He didn't like her. We all knew that."

"Who did Mr. Blume like?"

Objection. Again overruled.

"He liked the rest of us. He liked me, I know. And Jack. And Sarah. Everybody."

"Were there any young women in the class?"

"Sure. Lots of them."

"And how did Mr. Blume react to them?"

"Same as the rest of us. I mean, he watched them a lot, like any guy would. Are you asking me if he hit on the girls?"

"Yes. Exactly."

"I don't think so. I never heard anything about that. I never saw him talking to any of them alone. Sarah said he offered to help her get published. Jack told her to stay clear of Blume, Mr. Blume."

"Why would Jack say that? Jealousy?"

"Nah. Jack isn't jealous of anyone. He said Blume couldn't help anybody, or he'd have published more than he had."

I may have made a sound or some gesture. Billy blurted, "I'm sorry. I guess I didn't need to say that."

No, he didn't have to, but I don't blame him. When blows come, they just come and you take them.

After Billy's testimony, I wrote Carl Loeffle a note. "I don't mess around with my students, Carl. I want you to know that." He didn't respond, at least not then.

Sarah was spared testifying, since she had nothing to offer. It would have been hard on everyone.

Deputy Shirley Dyer was the best witness in a number of ways. He was casual, objective, down-home intelligent. I was probably the only person in the courtroom who realized how symmetrical he made my time in Mason, ushering me in, ushering me out. Maybe he knew, too. I imagine policemen dream about nets and webs. He confirmed each report read to him. Yes, they had found a small notepad in Nada's nightstand. The entry for that particular date was in Nada's handwriting. It read, "Volumes 1–12 to Dr.

Blume." She apparently kept records of everything. The same notepad, he said, had Blume's name by Volume 32 on an earlier date. There was no mention of any volumes being given to anyone else. As for the murder weapon, Dyer congenially reported, the laboratory had found minute, blue, cotton fibers on its surface. Matching fibers were found in the defendant's coat pocket. Fibers from the defendant's coat were found on the victim's coat. Dyer believed the defendant, Mr. Blume, disposed of the gloves. They might still turn up. And the notebooks—they were found at the Mason city dump, cut and torn to shreds. The defendant's fingerprints were not on any of them. They found none of the papers purported to be in the folders.

He agreed with my attorney that Nada could have disposed of the notebooks herself, or that someone else could have. But he believed I had done so. He seemed very content with that belief.

"She wrote that she had given 1–12 to Blume, and I think she did. Especially because of something Mr. Blume said the first time I came to his apartment."

"And what was that?"

"He said he knew she kept her writing in blue notebooks. It was tiny, and quick, but I wondered. How did he know they were all blue? Nobody knew that."

My attorney objected. No one knew for sure what color they had all been. Wasn't that correct? We only knew *some* of them were blue.

"And didn't you find something," the prosecutor asked, looking at the jury while he spoke to Dyer, "in the defendant's apartment that belonged to Miss Petrovich?"

"Yep. Found a key."

"A key to what?"

"Found a master key to the English Department. It was in a flat dish in the bathroom, along with some change and a paper clip. Only key there."

"And how do you know it was Nada Petrovich's key?"

"Because Miss Grace Burch said she had given such a key to Nada and it wasn't in the woman's purse. Miss Burch herself had marked the key rim with red nail polish. Just a dot. She said all the keys look alike, most of them don't have a number, so she color-codes them. And she had seen that particular key in Mr. Blume's bathroom the night before I went there. That's why, in fact, I went there myself."

With the exact timing of her kind, Margaret was in court for the brief period in which Deputy Dyer would validate both the existence and the origin of Nada's key. She had probably traded her lunch hour for this questionable victory. She sat on the back row and endeavored to keep her face behind the person in front of her. I knew where she was. The back pew had an unusual sheen from the sun, a rich burnished gold, and though I couldn't see Margaret, she was framed by that bright light. It was rather attractive.

Deputy Dyer was a credit to the sheriff's department. I imagine he hasn't stayed there.

But the star of the show was, as it should have been, Grace.

Grace sat Victorian erect, with her hands together in her lap. She looked at me often. Her determination was appealing. Most people fight what they can when they can.

"He was obsessed with Nada from the beginning," she said, "and I never could understand why. If Nada was around, he watched her. He worried that we were abusing her. He even went to the dean and chair about her."

"Why is that unusual? I mean, if Mr. Blume believed Nada was being taken advantage of, why shouldn't he try to correct the situation?"

"He should. It's just that he didn't want to accept that we had all tried to help Nada in some way, at some time. He wanted to be superior to us, to make us change our behavior for him. But he didn't actually do anything for her. Not that I know of."

"Such as what? Do what kind of things?"

"Well, I don't want to talk about my own charity. But we all sort of take—took—turns, during bad weather, for example, calling Nada at home, making sure her car was running. That's why I got her a master key. I knew she liked being in town, but I didn't want her staying with me, at the house. She liked having the run of the building, too. It gave her a sense of belonging, and a little pride around Margaret. Some of us sent her money every now and then, anonymously, of course. If Nada knew who did her a favor, she'd bow and scrape. . . ." She stopped, looked at her hands. Then she looked at the jury and resumed. "I'm sorry. She was a woman who tended to thank you to death." She stopped again. "His concern seemed extravagant, that's all."

"What did you yourself do for Nada? What was it you didn't want to mention?"

"It doesn't matter."

"Please."

"Well, I bought her a car, for one thing."

"You bought her a car?"

"Yes. It wasn't *new*. But it ran pretty well."

"And? Anything else?"

"I paid her stipend."

"And this means what? Explain for the court."

"Her assistantship contract ended last year. Every month I had a deposit made into her account—from my bank to hers—in the amount she would have earned. Sometimes a little more."

"Did she know this?"

"She asked me if I was the one doing it."

"And what did you say?"

"I lied. I told her no. If she'd been certain it came from me, she would have been my slave for life. She decided it was probably Dr. Harper, because he felt guilty. She said she was doing Dr. Harper a favor in return, that no one would ever know."

"Did Mr. Blume know any of this?"

"No. I told him a couple of times that people helped Nada, usually in secret. Once he said that was a coward's way of life."

Women just pick up little threads here and there, tie a knot or two, wander around weaving a mess no one can unravel.

"And how did he feel about Nada as a student? Her writing?"

"That's another thing. He was very concerned about Nada's writing ability. He asked me at least twice if I'd read her work. And he asked Carl Loeffle the same thing."

"How do you know this?"

"Carl was bothered that a new man, not even on tenure line, would do something *he* should have done. Then, later, after Nada's death, when I noticed her notebooks were missing, I wondered why anyone would want them. Arthur kept coming to mind." She touched her temple. "Arthur and Nada, Arthur and the notebooks. It scared me. It seemed outlandish, but it seemed right, too." She glanced at me and then at her hands. "I guess I knew all along. He had some odd ways. I thought he wasn't . . . normal, wasn't well."

The courtroom rustled like a stirring creature. People believed now would come the sordid, the unnatural. They didn't yet understand me and certainly didn't appreciate Grace. She wasn't one to spread ugliness. She ran from it.

"Explain precisely what you mean, Miss Burch."

"I'm referring primarily to his inability to look a woman in the eye and speak her name as if he knew who she was. He couldn't do that." She looked at me and so did most of the people I could see. "He can't do that," she added.

I could have right then, and have undone *her*. I chose not to. To do otherwise would have made her appear a liar.

"And he had a strong hostility toward our secretary. I think he may have tried to terrorize her, at least to worry her."

"Would you elucidate?"

She told of the missing cat, the collar, and then she mentioned the sketch. "Our secretary received it at her home and brought it to the office. She gave it to Dr. Walsh, who asked me, in confidence," she glanced at me then, as if to explain her betrayal, or what she probably believed was a betrayal, "if I thought Arthur, Mr. Blume, could have sent it to Margaret. I said, 'No.'"

"But you thought he had."

"I knew he had. I had seen that very sketch before, in the St. Louis train depot. Mr. Blume and I spent a day there and had ourselves drawn in caricature by a booth artist. That sketch was on display."

"Couldn't it have been a duplicate of a popular sketch?"

"Yes. And I hoped it was."

"But you lied to Dr. Walsh in order to protect Mr. Blume."

"Yes."

There was no way to reward her.

"Anything else, Miss Burch?"

"Yes. Nada herself said he was a troubled man and might be dangerous. She warned me to be careful."

"When was this?"

"Not long after he came."

"Did she say why?"

"No. She liked to drop hints about people, as if she knew something specific. It was her way of being important. I didn't need the warning, since I could see for myself he wasn't a very open man. I just didn't know the magnitude of what he was hiding."

The word "magnitude" astonished me, though I could hear in her inflection and see by her lips that she meant exactly that.

Magnitude.

Then I learned what Grace had done on Tuesday before coming to my place. She hadn't really suspected me. She had just known "something was wrong with the whole damned thing." She had been unable to rest at home, had been racked by guilt and a general anger. She had finally called the Mason police and, since small-town people can be obliging to one another, through them obtained the phone number of Nada's landlord. The landlord provided the key, but only to the sheriff, and when the sheriff and five of his men arrived at Nada's house, Grace was already there, waiting in her car. They let her come in the house but told her not to touch anything without permission. She wanted to let them know what might be out of place. Her little wolverine eyes probably didn't miss a thing. She roamed every room, mind just clicking away. Nothing in the house indicated anyone but Nada had been there. But Grace thought the bookcases looked odd. Two notebooks had fallen over. She thought Nada would have braced them with a bookend or something, and she said so. She made all her observations aloud, so the sheriff's men heard them—that Nada wouldn't travel in such weather; that if she *had* to do so, in an emergency, she would have called someone, she wouldn't have just skated out the door; that something was fishy here; that she had to find an address book so she could contact family or friends. And she wanted to take a dress for Nada. They wouldn't allow that yet, they told her. But later. She didn't want later. She was probably prim and contained, but bursting at the seams. Most men bend a little when women get like that. The deputies suggested she could possibly get names from the address book in Nada's purse. The sheriff called the station and advised them to allow Miss Burch to examine the belongings of Nada Petrovich. All by her dainty self, Grace had been calling the shots.

Grace left then, still astew, so much so that she turned the *wrong* way at the end of the road and had to make a U-turn a short distance up the highway. She worried that her car would get stuck. And she had, she said, an irrational fear that someone would be waiting for her if that happened. She headed back to town and passed the place where Nada's body had been found. She knew it must be the location, because the area was roped off and a patrol car was parked just off the pavement. She pulled behind the deputy's car and got out. He wouldn't let her inside the ropes. He chatted with her and they had a cigarette together. She kept looking around, not for anything in particular, just something. There were a number of broken tree limbs, twigs. But Grace's eyes lighted upon a stone that lay at the western edge of the roped area. It looked familiar.

"Could I see that stone?" she asked.

The deputy couldn't see it at first. They walked around the roped area, so Grace could look more closely.

And then she knew. Her heart sank and her legs went weak. It was a stone from Nada's house. She told him so and how she knew. He assured her he would tell the sheriff.

Grace was positive it came from Nada's because it had originally come from her. The stones had lined her house until she had the brick wall put in some months before. Nada had wanted the stones. She thought they were lovely.

See? A brick wall here, a stone wall there, and thus they seal the world.

Together, with Grace and a cadre of Midwestern minds, they conjectured that Nada had given a ride to someone, and that someone had been at the house and had taken along a stone from the flowerbed. When the coroner's report indicated that Nada had not received a death blow from falling, but from one wielded from above the ground, they fabricated possibilities. I, Grace told them, had shown an inordinate interest in Nada from the beginning of my term here. I had been fascinated with her writing. I had been in possession of at least one notebook. I had been in town during spring break.

So she went to my apartment. There, she had been convinced the folders on my bed held Nada's work. She was certain because the papers in the folders, at least in the one on top, were lined paper, and Nada used lined paper for her writing. Grace had never seen me do so. She didn't actually see the papers in the folder, but she could see the rounded edges, and thus knew the type of paper within. And, since the sheriff's office hadn't found any lined paper in my apartment, she was convinced it was Nada's work I was reading that night. She knew it that very night, especially after seeing the key. "I was terrified," she said. "There I was in the bathroom. The key was in plain sight and I could see him in the mirror. I thought he knew what I was thinking." Her gaze shifted to me. "I was afraid of him. I still am."

I shaped "Don't be" with my lips.

"And how," my attorney asked her, "did you know the defendant so well? That you would know so much about him?"

"We were friends."

"Intimate friends? Lovers?"

To her credit, she paused only long enough to take a deep breath. "Yes."

I was more relieved than I can explain, even to myself. She had said it aloud, in front of everyone.

"Didn't you tell the court, just moments ago, that you had suspicions all along?"

"Yes."

"But they didn't keep you from sleeping with Arthur Blume?"

The courtroom liked that question, the concreteness of it—that bodies still alive and in their view had been in the same bed together.

"I didn't suspect murder."

"What did you suspect?"

"I knew he didn't really like women. I thought perhaps I was an exception for him. That was vanity. I was also lonely and he was too. It's a human condition."

"Didn't you pursue Mr. Blume ardently and then feel rejected by him?"

I stood up then. "Please don't ask Dr. Burch any more questions." The judge waved his gavel, thought better of it, and ignored me. My attorney motioned me to sit down. He returned to Grace.

"Well?"

"Yes," she said. "More's the pity."

My attorney, satisfied and smiling, dismissed her and returned to sit by me.

"Good move," he said. "Defending her like that won you some points."

"I didn't do it for that reason," I said, but I don't think he believed me. A few moments later, I leaned to remind him that both Grace and Nada had introduced themselves to me. "They started everything." He didn't seem to think that was important.

My attorney didn't want me to go on the stand, but I insisted. It was my trial, after all. I wanted to be an active participant, not a sightseer. My testimony was direct, though the prosecutor hammered at me and accused me of playing word games.

"Did you go to the home of Nada Petrovich on the morning of March 12th?"

"No."

"You did leave your apartment that morning and drive somewhere?"

"Yes. I drove to campus for some books but was unable to get in the parking lot, due to ice. I then drove to the store for some cold medicine and tea and other things."

"And what time was this?"

"I believe it was about 10:00. It could have been a little earlier or later. I rarely notice time when I'm not in the classroom."

"Are you aware that Mr. Goff saw you leave the apartment building at 7:00 a.m.?"

"I know he believes he saw me at my car at that hour."

"And were you there?"

"I keep allergy pills in the glove compartment."

"Does that mean you were in your car for that purpose?"

"That's the only reason I can think of."

"Answer yes or no, Mr. Blume. Did you go to your car at 7:00 a.m. for cold medicine?"

"Not that I remember. I was quite ill at the time."

"Yes or no."

"No."

"Then why were you in your car?"

"I didn't say I was. I said that Jack believes I was."

And so on. My attorney advised me to answer directly and truthfully and I explained that I was doing so. After all, I didn't go to Nada's. I drove there. I visited. I checked on her. It wasn't her home—the house belonged to someone else. She had no home, no more than I did. She may have been born in another country. I didn't borrow the books. She didn't give them to me or lend them to me and I didn't take or steal them. There's no word for the transaction between us. If there were, and someone queried me accurately, I would say yes. The closest accurate description is that I won them. I never actually had them, never possessed them. I did once own blue gloves, but I wasn't sure where they were. For all I knew, they were in the hands of a stranger. If he had opened the box I mailed, he had Nada's manuscripts and my gloves, too. I certainly didn't have either.

Nada's death, too, wasn't my fault. The situation caused her death. I genuinely liked Nada. When I swung the branch, she still lived. She died sometime after that. I was gone by then. When the prosecutor asked, "Did you kill Nada Petrovich?" I responded "No." When he asked, "Did you take Nada Petrovich to an isolated spot and swing the branch that caused her death?" I said, "No." Why should I say yes? How could I? The spot was not isolated. It was on a major road. The branch didn't cause her death. It was an intermediary object only. As was I. Once he stared at me and growled, "Did you swing that branch, *that* branch, at Nada Petrovich's head?" and I said, "No." How could I be certain which branch they had brought in as evidence? He stepped nearer. He put his hands on the railing before the witness chair and said, "Did you swing any branch at Nada's head? Any at all?"

"I've already answered that," I said.

The judge leaned toward me. "Answer it again."

I told him the truth. "I can't answer any other way. I'm sorry. I've done the best I can."

The prosecutor grunted and turned away.

When they told me to step down, I turned toward the jury. I wanted to undo a damning impression left by the prosecution. "I've never touched one of my own students. I set rules for myself and I follow them. They're more demanding than any you set for me." I added, since my attorney hadn't, "And women introduce themselves to me."

Details not allowed in the courtroom were broadcast on the local and Kansas City stations, and appeared in numerous articles. The press transformed me, like many people before me, from a man to a monster, and Nada from an elderly, inquisitive, and somewhat meddling woman to a felled saint.

The papers reported that at each town where I had lived, a woman I had known was missing or had been found dead some years later, sometimes in an entirely different state. They named ten women, Juliette Preston among them. They also mentioned my mother's death: "A neighbor, Belle Wilson, thought Mrs. Blume's death was suspicious though it was termed 'accidental' on the death certificate. Arthur Blume was visiting at Mrs. Blume's home during the time. Her body was found in a creek on her rural property."

Some news passages I was pleased to read. "He was hard," one of my composition students said. "You had to be *good*. But he was fair." Dr. Walsh said they found "this all hard to believe. Blume seemed a dedicated teacher. We were glad to have him." I liked what Carl Loeffle remarked: "Arthur seemed a real nice fellow, soft-hearted and easy-going. A good teacher, too. The whole thing's a disgrace."

I agree.

My stay in Mason ended in April, when I was transferred to the state prison in Jefferson City. We drove over the very bridge from which I had once seen an apple-fresh girl near the river, on my entry to Mason, my fresh start. I had wished us both good fortune and I wondered how she had fared. It was a beautiful month each time, luscious and vibrant.

Reporters and detectives and attorneys kept asking me where bodies were and I told them there wasn't a spot on this earth that didn't hold a body if you dug deeply enough. They eventually settled into their guessing games and gave up on me. By then, however, I'd been contacted by my old publisher. The company wanted to reprint my first book, *Fathers*, and they were very interested in reconsidering my second, *Ghosts*. I couldn't have planned that.

Another spring; another beginning.

CHAPTER 27

I'm supposed to be in prison for life, but I don't find that sentence unbearable. This is a safe place, with physical comforts and even a touch of respect. There are few surprises if one is a keen observer of human nature, which is only one form of animal nature. I know whom to avoid, and when, and how to keep my eyes in the proper position as certain housemates pass. Survival in here is no different from survival in any community. One learns the rules.

In this hierarchy, I'm one of the elite, without having to admit to any qualifications. Whether or not I'm guilty matters far less than what I'm charged with: murder. It's much like having the right degree no matter the school attended. I may even warrant a higher status than I have, since sometimes the copier of a method is greater than the original master. But who can say when something is first done? And what if more than one master is copied? History gets rewritten when new facts or artifacts are uncovered. The creative mind finds many avenues of disguise and evasion. How else could it survive?

I don't really expect to stay here. Something will happen. It always does. An open door. A changed law. Perhaps science will explain motives and forgiveness will ensue.

I've started writing by hand now. That seems very appropriate to me, to take up Nada's method. I've earned it. I can feel the rightness of words in my hand and the beauty of letters as they flow from the pen. It fits the pattern.

Two weeks ago I received a small package containing a thin volume of verses by "Nada J. Petrovich." It was a handsome book: A scroll of pale lilies edged the blue binding; her name was in deep blue. The enclosed note read, "As you can see, we found some good stuff. I couldn't see any harm in sending this to you. Carl Loeffle." I wrote a thank-you that very day, and advised him that I was finishing my third book and already had a contract for it. "I've taken speculation a step further," I said, "as fiction is supposed to do." I signed it, "With fondness, AJB." I *am* fond of him. I'm fond of everyone there, except, of course, the Guardian of the Key. Margaret.

I settled down with the book after dinner. I lay on my cot and turned the desk lamp to light just the pages. The editors' page listed Grace Burch, Carl Loeffle, and, not surprisingly, William Butler, Jack Goff, and Sarah Fulkerson. That was very suitable, very right, all those names together with Nada's, holding her words firm for years to come. Clean little effort. The project was funded by Missouri Women in the Arts. I found that ironic, but also absolutely perfect. Her death made her work worthy of their support and attention. It was a respectable volume, too, seventy-three decent poems—a perfect number to those who knew her well. I think Nada would have liked the book and possibly wouldn't have begrudged the cost. She was old, after all, and that isn't easy to accept or endure.

I read the poems twice, then put the book with others on my wall unit. I wasn't certain where to place it—not on the top or second shelf, not next to Faulkner or Dostoevski, or Cervantes, or Fowles or Malamud. But not next to mine either. Finally I put it on the bottom shelf.

The next day I received my first marriage proposal. I'd been told that was likely to happen. It wouldn't have come as a surprise even if no one had warned me. I'll not accept, of course, though I don't need to refuse, either. I can outwait the desire. The woman sent me a photograph of herself and wrote that she'd like to visit me soon, so I could judge for myself that she wasn't a "mental case or anything." She believes I have been misjudged. She thinks I'm brilliant and talented and she would like to help me with my work. The photograph, which I realize may or may not be her, shows she's quite fair, with blonde hair billowing around a bovine face. Her eyebrows are strange, like quick strokes of a brown pencil. Her mouth, though, is pretty. Without the smile, it would be a smallish, rosebud mouth, so common among women. They may deliberately shape their lips that way, since a thin mouth is never considered attractive or sensual. I replied to her request with a definite yes, of course, do come, soon. She looks like a woman willing to work and to run errands. She wants to ease my path. I'll allow her to do so, and reward her as I may. I asked the woman to continue corresponding with me. "I like letters," I said. "They help one to construct an outside reality." She'll probably quote me from here to kingdom come. I doubt she will matter to me.

I'm lonely, admittedly. But I've always been lonely. I miss Grace. I wonder if she would believe that? I miss the presence of her and the possibility of her. I can hear her voice in this very place if I listen closely, especially in the night. It's like a light flickering on and off, on and off. Here. Over here. No, here.

Sometimes I see her, too, not in person, of course. She has never even written, though I've sent her cards and a few letters. I see her in my mind's eye, that deep memory that saves all that is important to our nature. It allows me glimpses of her. She is lovely, young and unblemished, ethereal, fading in and out, then settling still so I may look at her. She wears a classic white gown and picks at the lace bodice with her tiny fingers. Behind her is the door to her basement. It frames her well, a looming dark shadow.

She is a good woman, I know, with good motives. But then we all think we're doing right. I would like to visit her.

I often listen to and read analyses of my work and through them, more analyses of me. Now they conjecture as much about my mother as they do me. Such people amaze me. Where were they all that time? Mr. Watson has been quoted a great deal, which I understand. He puts people at ease. He used the word "pathetic" about my mother and me. I thought that was a poor word choice, but I understood his reasons. "Arthur was the saddest kid," Mr. Watson said. "He used to look at people with such longing, but we didn't know what to do for him. We didn't know what he wanted. I helped as much as I could. I offered him goods from the store but he wouldn't take them. He was such a hungry little pup."

I hated that analogy. I'm grander than that, surely. Any human is. And of course I didn't take his charity. My mother was a proud woman and I'm her son. She wasn't all bad, any more than I am. She loved me. She took madness as her lot and she lived with it and she raised me in spite of demons hounding her from all sides. She was brave. I hope I'm brave.

Sometimes I'm so taken with the irony of this situation. *I* am the one imprisoned in a tower.

I'm already planning my next book. I have to write it because it has become a part of me and I have to give it life. It will have a single narrator, a charming young woman named Rose. It will, I imagine, given the nature of the character and the voice I've discovered, be a romance. I'm going to dedicate it to my mother and all the women of the world, and sign it as I sign below.

Always,
Arthur J. Blume

Writing Arthur Blume

When I first thought to write about my experience with a serial killer, I believed that in addition to the gift of survival—for which I was and am most grateful—the encounter had been a gift of story. It was so full of irony, close calls, ridiculous mistakes, that I had only to hold the pen—figuratively—and a bestseller would flow onto the page. I had been married to a policeman for twenty years. My ex-husband was a homicide detective. He had met the murderer. He had seen the televised feature on Robert Weeks. He was the arresting detective. Oh, rich stuff. I saved notes, letters, transcribed phone calls. I was ready.

But the book wouldn't work. It was absolute torture to write. There were twists and turns that weren't right or true no matter how accurate they were. Weeks was interesting *because* he had killed women, not because of any outstanding characteristics. Certainly, he seemed an absolute gentleman, well read, with old-world charm, intelligence, a good education, and nice outward form. But he was also boring and slick, with perspectives that a woman in an intimate situation may notice but not believe could possibly be dangerous. He didn't mention names, dates, places. His world was generic; his past was amorphous. He called me "Pretty Lady" even after repeated requests that he not do so. His pat phrases, such as "We'll have our time, our time will come," took on meaning only *after* I learned he was a murderer.

While our little community had been dealing with the surface Weeks, there was another one, the one watching, perhaps planning vengeance, perhaps not planning at all, just waiting. That was the one I wanted to write about and I couldn't do it. I only knew him as he had wanted to be known. In addition to their depraved wants, many serial killers, at least the ones who've been caught, want fame. Once he was in prison, Robert Weeks wanted me to help him write a book, or to help me succeed through him, which tainted even the thought of telling his story directly. I had to learn more and to let it settle inside me in a way that allowed a whole person to form. Through me, his legacy would not be to sensationalize and romanticize violent acts, making them worthy of remembrance, but rather to help explain the human condition, the paradox between the good neighbor and his evil acts.

Over the years, I've done that, and my character, Arthur Blume, took shape. There are similarities between Weeks and Blume, but Blume is ultimately far more real to me, far more human, because I've filled in the gaps and I feel sorry for him. I've read about killers until I'm embarrassed to admit the details I know. There's a discontinuity in the aberrant mind, and if we want the truth about serial killers we have to approach it slant (a twist on Dickinson), because that's how they tell it. The reporters who interviewed Ted Bundy had to talk to him about what the murderer *might* have done. They had to ask him to conjecture—and they believed his conjecturing. My acquaintance, Weeks, wouldn't—or couldn't—say he wasn't a murderer. He talked in clues, roundabout paths. "I believe you were going to kill me," I said. "No," Weeks replied, drawing it out like a sigh.

Serial killers *appear* normal because in many ways they are. Only in hindsight do we recognize that little clues were monstrous signs. Arthur Blume's innuendoes, gaps, seeming passivity, inability to respond directly to certain types of questions, are common traits among serial killers. They've got terrible secrets (Dahmer killed and tortured animals as a young child; Ted Bundy watched his grandfather read pornography; Bundy came into his aunt's room holding a butcher knife; Arthur was abused), but they don't evaluate their experiences the same way we do. Throughout *An Absolute Gentleman*, Blume demonstrates the unusual reasoning that will take him through the trial, believing that he is truthful. His kindnesses and grace are genuine; he can care about someone and then kill them— like the white tiger in a magician's show, just with a bit more finesse.

I have always been fascinated by the animal kingdom, and all of Blume's examples of aberrant behavior in the animal world are factual, drawn from nature shows, magazines such as *Discover, Science,* or *Nature*, and books by writers such as Carl Sagan, Desmond Morris, Robert Arbrey, Lewis Thomas, and Stephen J. Gould, but especially from documentaries. One documentary described a crazed female chimp that stole others' infants, ate them, and taught her daughter to do the same. When the mother died, the younger female stopped the behavior. Another documentary explored the ape that didn't know how to nurture. Increasingly, our culture tries to understand humans by studying animals. We hope through understanding we can gain control, over ourselves, our environment, over our fears. So does Blume.

Even with the proliferation of popular crime dramas on television and America's obsession with reality shows, or perhaps because of them, truth seems stranger than fiction. We can lock our doors from strangers, we can avoid bad neighborhoods and dark alleys, but how do we protect ourselves and our loved ones from the charming co-worker, the timid schoolboy, or the church rector, from the Scott Petersons, Ted Bundys, and BTKs? Jack the Ripper has been memorialized for more than a century, and yet we continue to fall victim to his successors. We may watch our backs for a while, but we get drawn in like victims of a tsunami, chasing the receding waters before the wave rather than running for higher ground.

After identifying Weeks from an episode of *Unsolved Mysteries* and maintaining a relationship with him in prison at the suggestion of my ex-husband, I sought assurance of safety from a police psychiatrist. He advised me that one can't predict what a serial killer will do, and thus there is no way to guard against one, no way to be safe. The exact example given was that the psychotic may wake and decide today he will kill Helen Dogood from ten or fifteen years ago. He may not know why. But if he decides, he'll act on it. Something that gets in his way may deter him—that's not predictable either—but the sight on the victim may rise again. Blume suddenly becomes aware of the victim—through proximity, or through some innocuous reminder. His victims *come* to him—they are presented or suggested by something outside his control. He lives among us as friend, colleague, neighbor, nice guy, and surprises us—but not totally—by being, simultaneously, murderer.

R.M. Kinder